COMPACT TRAINING

Fit for
Business English

Verkaufsgespräche

Robert Tilley

Bisher sind in dieser Reihe erschienen:

- Fit for Business English – Telefonieren
- Fit for Business English – Korrespondenz
- Fit for Business English – Verkaufsgespräche
- Fit for Business English – Präsentationen

Weitere Titel sind in Vorbereitung.

© 2001 Compact Verlag München
Alle Rechte vorbehalten. Nachdruck,
auch auszugsweise, nur mit ausdrücklicher
Genehmigung des Verlages gestattet.
Chefredaktion: Ilse Hell
Redaktion: Karina Partsch
Redaktionsassistenz: Katharina Eska, Damla Özbay,
Alexandra Pawelczak, Stefanie Sommer
Fachredaktion: Ted Hall, Anthony Moore
Übersetzung: Marc Hillefeld
Produktionsleitung: Gunther Jaich
Gestaltung: Hendryk Sommer

ISBN 3-8174-7163-7
7271631

Besuchen Sie uns im Internet: www.compactverlag.de

Vorwort

Englisch ist die länderübergreifende Sprache der Wirtschaft. Angesichts der zunehmenden Globalisierung der Märkte werden gute Englischkenntnisse immer wichtiger für den beruflichen Erfolg.

Die Reihe **Fit for Business English** ermöglicht dem Benutzer die zielgerechte Vorbereitung auf verschiedene Themenbereiche des modernen Wirtschaftsenglisch.

Der Band **Fit for Business English – Verkaufsgespräche** trainiert speziell die Kommunikation bei Verkaufsverhandlungen. Dabei wird gezeigt, wie man in englischer Sprache Kunden akquiriert, Produkte präsentiert, Angebote unterbreitet und Vertragsbedingungen aushandelt.

Dies geschieht anhand einer Story: Der Deutsche Peter Brückner wird von seiner Firma nach England versetzt. Um den nötigen Lernspaß zu garantieren, werden seine Erlebnisse in humorvoller Weise dargestellt.

Alle Dialoge sind praxisnah und sowohl in englischer Sprache als auch in der deutschen Übersetzung angegeben. Die Schlüsselbegriffe sind im Text farbig hervorgehoben.

Nach jedem Dialog folgen zur Überprüfung und Vertiefung des gelernten Wortschatzes kurze Übungen. Die Lösungen sind im Anhang zu finden.

Sprachpraktische und kulturelle Besonderheiten werden an gegebener Stelle angemerkt. Hierzu gehören Tipps zum korrekten Sprachgebrauch sowie landeskundliche Hinweise.

Verschiedene Symbole zu Beginn jedes Abschnitts erleichtern dem Benutzer den Zugriff auf die für ihn relevanten Passagen.

Am Ende jedes Kapitels werden alle wichtigen Vokabeln und Redewendungen nochmals angeführt.

Mit einem abschließenden Test im Anhang kann der Leser seinen Kenntnisstand überprüfen.

Inhalt

Vorwort	3
Story	5
Kunden akquirieren	6
Produkte präsentieren	29
Geschäftsabschlüsse erzielen	53
Angebote unterbreiten	82
Vertragsbedingungen aushandeln	110
Test	134
Auf einen Blick: Redewendungen rund ums Verkaufen	137
Glossar	143
Lösungen	149

 Here we go: kleine Einleitung am Anfang des Kapitels

 Talk Talk Talk: praxisnahe Dialoge mit deutschen Übersetzungen, die wichtigsten Stichwörter sind farbig markiert

 Train Yourself: abwechslungsreiche Übungen trainieren den gelernten Wortschatz

 Background Information: Wissenswertes zu Business und Landeskunde

 Do's and Don'ts: Tipps zum korrekten Verhalten in Geschäftssituationen

 False Friends: Hinweise auf mögliche sprachliche Fehler

 Vocabulary: Vokabelliste mit dem Wortschatz des Kapitels

 The Test: Im Abschlusstest zeigt es sich: Was haben Sie gelernt? Wo sind vielleicht noch Ihre Schwächen?

 Ready to talk: Alles Wichtige zum Nachschlagen

 Glossary: Zusammenfassung aller neuen Vokabeln

 Solutions: Die Lösungen zu Übungen im Text und zum Abschlusstest

Story

Peter Brückner ist 30 Jahre alt. Nach seinem BWL-Studium wurde er als Assistent des Vertriebsleiters bei der internationalen Firma ERGO Ltd. beschäftigt. ERGO Ltd. ist ein innovatives Unternehmen und hat sich auf die Produktion von Zubehörteilen im IT-Bereich spezialisiert.

Um Peter Brückner auf eine spätere Führungsposition vorzubereiten, wird er in die Filiale nach London versetzt, um dort die Abläufe des internationalen Vertriebs kennen zu lernen. Wie viele andere Unternehmen, legt auch ERGO Ltd. großen Wert darauf, dass künftige Führungskräfte Auslandserfahrungen sammeln.

Dieser Band der Reihe **Fit for Business English** zeigt, wie Peter Brückner erfolgreich Verkaufsgespräche in englischer Sprache führt.
Tatkräftige Unterstützung erhält er dabei von seinen neuen Kollegen, die ihm jederzeit mit nützlichen Tipps zur Seite stehen und ihn auf die kulturellen und sprachlichen Feinheiten hinweisen. Dies sind:
– James Morgan, Managing Director, direkter Vorgesetzter von Peter
– Steve Blackman, Leiter der Verkaufsabteilung
– Melissa Walker, Marketing Managerin
– Lucy Scott, Sekretärin und »gute Seele« des Büros.

Schon bald ist Peter Brückner mit den wichtigsten Strategien vertraut und weiß, wie man in englischer Sprache Argumente einbringt und Verkaufsgespräche führt. Um seine Kenntnisse noch weiter auszubauen, erhält er die Möglichkeit, mit seinem Kollegen Steve Blackman an einem Verkaufsseminar teilzunehmen. Auf einer anschließenden Geschäftsreise kann Peter sein Wissen in die Praxis umsetzen und verhilft ERGO Ltd. zu einem erfolgreichen Geschäftsabschluss.

Acquire customers
Kunden akquirieren

 **Here we go**

Nachdem Peter sich schon in viele Bereiche bei seiner Firma ERGO Limited eingearbeitet hat, ist sein Vorgesetzter James Morgan nun der Überzeugung, dass Peter sich näher mit der Verkaufsabteilung von Steve Blackman befassen sollte. Er muss sich jetzt Gedanken darüber machen, wie man eine Verkaufsstrategie am besten angeht und wie man Menschen dazu animiert, ein Produkt zu kaufen. Seine ersten Versuche startet er sogleich bei seinen eigenen Kollegen ...

 Talk Talk Talk

(James Morgan's office at ERGO Limited, Peter Brückner enters)

J. Good morning, Peter! Did you have a good weekend?

P. Very enjoyable, Mr Morgan. I spent it with my friends in Sussex, again.

J. Not hunting, surely?

P. No, the season's over. We drove down to Brighton.

J. And what do you think of Brighton? It's been **run down** so much recently in the press.

(James Morgans Büro bei ERGO Limited. Peter Brückner tritt ein)

J. Guten Morgen, Peter! Hatten Sie ein schönes Wochenende?

P. Ich habe es sehr genossen, Mr. Morgan. Ich habe es wieder mit meinen Freunden in Sussex verbracht.

J. Aber Sie haben doch nicht wieder gejagt?

P. Nein, die Saison ist vorüber. Wir sind runter nach Brighton gefahren.

J. Und was halten Sie von Brighton? In der Presse wurde in letzter Zeit viel **darüber hergezogen**

P. Actually, I liked the place very much. It's got – what do you say, a **buzz**? Probably because of all the university students.

J. Brighton also knows how to sell itself – and that brings me to what I want to talk to you about, Peter. I'd like you to **immerse yourself** during the next few weeks in our **sales operation** and then report to me on your ideas on **how we could improve things in that area**.

P. Certainly, Mr Morgan, but what do you want me to do?

J. Steve Blackman's going down to the West Country next week for an **intensive seminar** in **salesmanship**. I'd like you to go with him. He's following that up with a tour of our **sales offices**. I'd like you write that down in your **schedule**, too.

P. Also eigentlich gefiel mir der Ort sehr gut. Er – wie sagt man – **er brummt**? Wahrscheinlich wegen all der Studenten von der Universität.

J. Brighton versteht es außerdem, sich selbst zu verkaufen – und genau darüber wollte ich mit Ihnen sprechen, Peter. Ich möchte, dass Sie sich während der nächsten paar Wochen **intensiv in unsere Verkaufsaktivitäten einarbeiten** und mir dann über Ihre Ideen berichten, **wie wir diesen Bereich noch verbessern könnten**.

P. Natürlich, Mr. Morgan, aber was genau soll ich tun?

J. Steve Blackman fährt nächste Woche für ein **Intensiv-Seminar** über das **Verkaufsgeschäft** hinunter ins West Country. Ich möchte, dass Sie ihn begleiten. Er macht danach eine Tour zu unseren **Verkaufsbüros**. Ich möchte, dass Sie auch das in Ihren **Terminkalender** eintragen.

Colloquial English

Peter says that Brighton has got a **buzz**. This means it has a **lively atmosphere**.
Also: The place was **buzzing**.
»To **give someone a buzz**« means **to telephone**.

Background Information

Many verbs in English include the prepositions »**up**« and »**down**«. Some such as »**drive up/down**« and »**go up/down**« have a literal sense of direction, i.e. Brighton is south of London, so Peter drove down to Brighton just as he would drive up to Edinburgh. Similarly, one would go up the mountain and then down again.

Others such as »**run down**« (generally used to mean »to discredit somebody or something«) have no obvious literal meaning. »To **write down**« means to make a note of something, or to copy something, »to **write up**«, on the other hand implies a longer process, e.g. »I'm writing up my reports at the moment«; direction has nothing to do with it.

Some other »up/down« phrasal verbs include:
to put up	to give accommodation to somebody
to put down	to belittle or make somebody feel inferior
to set up	to establish, install
to bring up	to introduce a new idea, to mention
to scale down	to reduce
to let down	to disappoint
to turn down	to reject or refuse

Train Yourself

Setzen Sie das korrekte »phrasal verb« in die folgenden Sätze ein.
Verwenden Sie folgende Begriffe: *run down, write down, write up, follow up, set up, scale down, let down, put up, put down, go up, go down, turn down*.
1. The management are ▓▓▓▓▓▓▓▓▓▓ operations in Eastern Europe and making many employees redundant.
2. Can you ▓▓▓▓▓▓▓▓ this ▓▓▓▓▓▓▓▓ please, Lucy, it's for a speech I'm preparing for the conference this weekend.
3. I think it's important to ▓▓▓▓▓▓▓▓ the subject of overtime in next week's meeting.

4. Where are you staying?
   Oh, they're ▒▒▒▒ me ▒▒▒▒ in the Hilton Hotel, would you believe!
5. We're ▒▒▒▒ a new franchise agreement to boost sales in the American market.
6. We don't want to ▒▒▒▒ Rothmans ▒▒▒▒! We told them our report would be there today! Send this express post immediately!
7. Peter ▒▒▒▒ his presentation with a quick tour of the department.
8. Simon was ▒▒▒▒ for the position of general manager. He was devastated.
9. Why are you so tired?
   I spent all night ▒▒▒▒ the new proposals for the merger.
10. He's not a popular member of the department because he's always ▒▒▒▒ colleagues behind their backs.
11. We can ▒▒▒▒ to Manchester tonight. It's only a two hour drive from London.
12. I'm ▒▒▒▒ to the shops! Does anybody want something?

Talk Talk Talk

(Peter's office. Steve Blackman enters)

(Peters Büro. Steve Blackman tritt ein)

S. Come on Peter, **drop what you're doing** and follow me to my office – the *Nag's Head*. Buy me a beer and I'll tell you all you need to know about selling!

S. Kommen Sie, Peter – **lassen Sie alles stehen und liegen** und folgen Sie mir in mein Büro – ins *Nag's Head*. Spendieren Sie mir ein Bier und ich verrate Ihnen alles übers Verkaufen, was Sie wissen müssen!

P. I **gather** we're off on a **sales trip** together. That should be fun.

P. Ich **habe gehört**, dass wir zusammen auf eine **Verkaufsreise** gehen. Das wird bestimmt ein Spaß.

S. Don't count on it, Peter my dear chap ...	S. Erhoffen Sie sich nicht zu viel, Peter, alter Freund ...
(In the pub) S. So what's it to be?	(Im Pub) S. Also, was darf's sein?
P. Oh, make mine a pint of best bitter – there's nothing waiting for me on my desk today.	P. Oh, ich nehme ein Pint *Best Bitter* – auf meinem Schreibtisch wartet heute keine Arbeit mehr auf mich.
S. Now, did the **old man** fill you in?	S. Also, hat **der Alte** Sie ins Bild gesetzt?
P. He said we'd be attending a sales seminar and then touring our **sales points** around the country.	P. Er hat mir gesagt, dass wir an einem Verkaufsseminar teilnehmen und dann unsere **Verkaufsstellen** in der Umgebung abklappern.
S. You're in for a grand tour. We start in Bournemouth – that's where the seminar is being held. Then we head for Plymouth, from where we cover the West Country. Then over to Cardiff, to see how Wales is being covered. Then up to Scotland, to Glasgow and Edinburgh. And all in two weeks. You'll need a holiday after that.	S. Machen Sie sich auf eine große Tour gefasst. Wir starten in Bournemouth – dort wird das Seminar abgehalten. Dann fahren wir weiter nach Plymouth, von wo aus wir das West Country abdecken. Dann rüber nach Cardiff, um zu sehen, wie Wales abgedeckt wird. Dann geht es hoch nach Schottland, nach Glasgow und Edinburgh. Und das alles in zwei Wochen. Danach werden Sie urlaubsreif sein.
P. Well, I was planning to get back to Hamburg for a short visit ...	P. Tja, ich hatte sowieso vor, für einen Kurzbesuch zurück nach Hamburg zu gehen ...

Background Information

The devolution of regional political powers in Britain in 1999 – giving Scotland its own Parliament and Wales a semi-autonomous National Assembly – led to a **boost** in business activity in Glasgow, Edinburgh and Cardiff. Many companies strengthened their presence in Wales and Scotland in anticipation of greater investment there.

Train Yourself

Steve sagt zu Peter, er solle alles stehen und liegen lassen. Er verwendet dabei den Ausdruck »drop what you're doing« im Sinne von »stop doing what you're doing right now«. Im Englischen gibt es viele solcher umgangssprachlicher Redewendungen. **Finden Sie nun heraus, was nachstehende Wendungen bedeuten!**

1. Drop in and see us.
....
2. Drop me a line.
....
3. Just another drop!
....
4. A drop-out.
....
5. Drop off to sleep.
....
6. Drop something off.
....

Talk Talk Talk

(Peter's office. Melissa Walker enters)

M. **Off on your travels again**, Peter, I hear!

(Peters Büro. Melissa Walker tritt ein)

M. Ich habe gehört, **Sie brechen schon wieder zu einer Reise auf**, Peter!

P. A bit further **afield** this time, Melissa. I shall actually get to see Wales and Scotland.

M. You'll love Scotland. Every German I ever met **fell** for the country. My German teacher was **wild about** Edinburgh. She told me nearly every Scottish city, town and village is twinned with a partner in Bavaria.

P. I'm also looking forward to seeing Wales.

M. Do you know, I've never been there. But the countryside around Snowdon and the other mountains is supposed to be beautiful.

P. Melissa, **when it comes to selling** a place I think I could learn a lot from you!

M. Don't laugh, Peter, but I once worked in marketing for the National Tourist Board! But I left before I could get to Wales …

P. Diesmal geht es etwas weiter **hinaus**, Melissa. Ich werde tatsächlich Wales und Schottland sehen.

M. Schottland wird Ihnen gefallen. Jeder Deutsche, den ich bis jetzt kennen gelernt habe, **hat sich** in das Land dort **verliebt**. Meine Deutschlehrerin war ganz versessen auf Edinburgh. Sie hat mir erzählt, dass fast jede schottische Stadt und jedes Dorf eine Partnerstadt in Bayern hat.

P. Ich freue mich auch darauf, Wales zu sehen.

M. Wissen Sie, ich war nie da. Aber die Landschaft um Snowdon und die anderen Berge müssen wirklich wunderschön sein.

P. Melissa, **wenn es darum geht**, eine Gegend **anzupreisen**, könnte ich eine Menge von Ihnen lernen.

M. Lachen Sie nicht, Peter, aber ich habe einmal im Marketing für das Nationale Touristenbüro gearbeitet! Aber ich bin von dort weggegangen, bevor ich je nach Wales gekommen bin …

Background Information

Twinning: Several regions in Great Britain have developed strong business ties to German states through twinning arrangements between cities and towns in both countries. A special relationship has arisen in this way between Scotland and Bavaria, where 20 cities and towns are twinned with Scottish communities. The most notable are the twinnings of Munich and Edinburgh, Nuremberg and Glasgow.

False Friends

Melissa asks »**Off on your travels?**« meaning »**Are you leaving to go travelling?**«. Saying to somebody »**Right, I'm off! See you later!** « is very common in English. (Be careful, however, you don't get confused with the meaning of »**off**« to describe rotten food! e.g. »Urgh! **This meat is off! It stinks!**«)

There are also several verbs which use the preposition »**off**«:

to call off	to cancel
to put off	to postpone
to take off	to increase rapidly
to pull off	to succeed in something
to set off	to start a journey
to switch off	to begin to relax

Train Yourself

Füllen Sie die Lücken mit oben stehenden »phrasal verbs«:
1. The deal was ▅▅▅▅ when the managing director suddenly resigned.
2. We ▅▅▅▅ in a hurry because Jonathon couldn't find his passport.
3. Everyone was delighted that we ▅▅▅▅ the deal so quickly. We expected the negotiations to take much longer.
4. During the last quarter sales have really ▅▅▅▅ and profits are up by 40 per cent.
5. The meeting was ▅▅▅▅ until next week when everybody could attend.
6. Due to the pressures of work it is vital to ▅▅▅▅ every now and again.

Background Information

Melissa also says, »**Every German I ever met fell for the country**«. This does not mean they fell down and hurt themselves but rather they had a strong initial liking for the country. The meaning is virtually the same as to fall in love.

Other phrases with »**for**« are:

to make up for	to compensate for
to make for	to result in
to bargain for	to take into account
to stand for	to represent (i.e. initials)
to put in for	to apply for

Train Yourself

Wählen Sie die passenden »phrasal verbs« aus oben stehender Liste für die folgenden Sätze!

1. We hadn't ▬▬▬▬▬▬ stiff competition from our rivals and our sales reflected this.
2. The BBC ▬▬▬▬▬▬ British Broadcasting Corporation.
3. Did you hear? Tony's ▬▬▬▬▬▬ the new management position. I hope he gets it.
4. She visited the new location for the company's offices and ▬▬▬▬▬▬ it immediately. It was perfect.
5. The Internet ▬▬▬▬▬▬ much easier communication with potential customers all over the world.
6. The success of the new prototype ▬▬▬▬▬▬ all the disappointments of the past.

Talk Talk Talk

(Peter arrives at the office the next day. Lucy Scott, the secretary, greets him)

(Am nächsten Tag kommt Peter im Büro an. Lucy Scott, die Sekretärin, begrüßt ihn)

L. Good morning, Peter. You're off for a grand tour of the country, I hear!	L. Guten Morgen, Peter. Ich habe gehört, Sie brechen zu einer großen Tour durch das Land auf!
P. **News does travel fast**, Lucy!	P. **Neuigkeiten verbreiten sich hier schnell**, Lucy!
L. Well, I should be the first to know – I'm making all the **travel arrangements** for you and Steve!	L. Tja, ich sollte auch die Erste sein, die das erfährt – schließlich treffe ich die **Reisevorbereitungen** für Sie und Steve!
P. Lucy, for the next few days, until we leave, I'm going to use you as a **guinea-pig**, if you don't mind, to help me **prepare for the seminar**. I know nothing about salesmanship.	P. Lucy, wenn Sie nichts dagegen haben, werde ich Sie in den nächsten paar Tagen vor unserer Abreise als **Versuchskaninchen** missbrauchen, um mich **auf das Seminar vorzubereiten**. Ich weiß überhaupt nichts über das Verkaufsgeschäft.
L. Nor do I, Peter!	L. Genau so wenig wie ich, Peter!
P. But you buy things – so in that sense you're an expert in salesmanship. For instance, what **considerations make you decide** to buy one product rather than another?	P. Aber Sie kaufen Dinge ein – in diesem Sinne sind sie eine Expertin im Verkaufsgeschäft. **Wie** zum Beispiel **treffen Sie eine Entscheidung** darüber, ein bestimmtes Produkt statt einem anderen zu kaufen?
M. (enters) That's my area, Peter. Marketing.	M. (tritt ein) Das ist mein Fachgebiet, Peter. Marketing.
P. But **the two areas coincide**, don't they?	P. Aber **diese beiden Gebiete überschneiden sich**, oder?
L. Look, this is getting too complicated for me. Tea, anyone?	L. Also das wird mir jetzt zu kompliziert. Möchte jemand Tee?

P. Now there's an example! Tea! What makes you buy that **brand** in preference to another, Lucy?

M. But that's a supermarket product that sells itself through **clever packaging** and marketing. Salesmanship has nothing to do with it.

P. Well, perhaps in this case not. But haven't you ever been approached in the supermarket or in a department store by a **sales representative** asking you to **try out a certain product**?

L. You're right. It happened to me this morning. There was a **stand** at the entrance to the food hall of our local department store and biscuits were being **handed out**.

P. Handed out, Lucy? Did everybody accept a biscuit?

L. Well, no. I didn't, for instance.

P. Why not?

L. I didn't like the look of the young girl handing them out. And she just sort of threw them at people!

P. There you have it! A bad **sales-**

P. Ein gutes Beispiel! Tee! Warum kaufen Sie diese **Marke** statt einer anderen, Lucy?

M. Aber das ist ein Produkt aus dem Supermarkt, das sich selbst durch eine **clevere Verpackung** und Marketing verkauft. Verkaufsgeschick hat damit überhaupt nichts zu tun.

P. Gut, in diesem Fall vielleicht nicht. Aber ist in einem Supermarkt oder Kaufhaus denn nie ein **Verkäufer** an Sie herangetreten und hat Ihnen angeboten, **ein bestimmtes Produkt auszuprobieren**?

L. Sie haben Recht. Das ist mir erst heute Morgen passiert. Am Eingang der Lebensmittelabteilung unseres Kaufhauses war ein **Stand** aufgebaut, an dem Kekse **verteilt** wurden.

P. Verteilt, Lucy? Hat denn jeder ein Keks angenommen?

L. Tja, nein. Ich zum Beispiel nicht.

P. Warum nicht?

L. Mir gefiel nicht, wie das junge Mädchen, das sie verteilte, aussah. Und sie hat sie den Leuten regelrecht aufgezwungen!

P. Da haben Sie es! Schlechtes

person. Sloppy appearance and personal presentation and no motivation.	**Verkaufspersonal. Schlampiges Erscheinungsbild, schlechte Präsentation und keine Motivation.**
M. Wow, Peter! Do you really need to go to that seminar?	M. Wow, Peter! Müssen Sie wirklich noch an diesem Seminar teilnehmen?

Background Information

Peter asks Lucy in this section if she doesn't mind being used as a **guinea-pig** to help him prepare for a seminar. A »**guinea-pig**«, as well as being a small furry animal, can also refer to a person used in a scientific experiment, and this is obviously the meaning Peter has in mind.

There are many other words and expressions in English that refer to **testing/experimentation** and some are listed below:

to sound out	(colloquial) to discover somebody's intentions or opinions
to try out	to test something in order to see how useful or effective it is
to pilot	to judge how good something is before introducing it
to test the water	(colloquial) to find out people's opinions before introducing something
a prototype	The first example of something from which later forms are developed.
a sample	an example, usually given free, of an article or commodity being offered for sale so that possible buyers can examine or test it
a trial run	a practical test of something new, or unknown, to discover its effectiveness
a pitch	persuasive talk or arguments for financial gain

Train Yourself

Benutzen Sie die oben aufgeführten Wendungen (einschließlich »guinea-pig«) um die folgenden Lücken zu füllen. Verwenden Sie dabei jeden Begriff nur einmal!

1. Have you seen the ▬▬▬▬▬ of the new Amstrad computer? They're hoping to move into mass production with it next year.
2. I hear you're off to that sales conference in Paris next week. I don't know yet, I've got to ▬▬▬▬▬ it ▬▬▬▬▬ with the boss first.
3. The company is venturing the Eastern European market to ▬▬▬▬▬ the new product.
4. They made several ▬▬▬▬▬ in the domestic sector before launching the product abroad.
5. As I was saying, Peter, I need to ▬▬▬▬▬ with this one before we go ahead with production.
6. They're asking for students to be used as ▬▬▬▬▬ in their research into the common cold.
7. They're ▬▬▬▬▬ a new brand of biscuit in my local supermarket.
8. There are sales people handing out ▬▬▬▬▬ on every aisle.
9. The representative gave his sales ▬▬▬▬▬ about quality and quantity.

 **Talk Talk Talk**

(Beryl, Melissa's assistant, peeps into Peter's office)

P. Good morning, Beryl. Care to join us in this illuminating conversation?

B. So what are you lot chatting about?

(Beryl, Melissas Assistentin, wirft einen Blick in Peters Büro)

P. Guten Morgen, Beryl. Möchten Sie unserer erhellenden Diskussion nicht beitreten?

B. Über was quasselt ihr denn hier?

M. Selling, Beryl. Peter here is getting all **geared up** for that seminar he'll be attending with Steve.

P. Beryl, when did you last buy anything because of a **convincing sales pitch**? And what did you buy?

B. Let me see ... Well, funnily enough, I bought some lens-cleaning liquid from a **sales stand** in that shopping mall of Leicester Square only yesterday.

P. Lens-cleaning liquid?

B. You know the stuff. You clean your spectacles with it. Or a camera lens.

M. Good lord! But why did you buy that Beryl? You don't even wear spectacles!

B. I wear sunglasses, and they get very dirty here in London.

P. But why did you buy the liquid? That's what I'd like to know.

B. The young man **made a very good sales pitch. He made out a**

M. Über das Verkaufsgeschäft, Beryl. Unser Peter bereitet sich auf das Seminar vor, an dem er zusammen mit Steve teilnehmen wird.

P. Beryl, wann haben Sie das letzte Mal etwas wegen einer **überzeugenden Verkaufsstrategie** gekauft? Und was?

B. Mal sehen ... tja, komischerweise habe ich gestern eine Linsen-Reinigungsflüssigkeit an einem **Verkaufsstand** gekauft, der in dem Einkaufscenter am Leicester Square aufgebaut war.

P. Linsen-Reinigungsflüssigkeit?

B. Sie kennen doch dieses Zeug. Man kann damit seine Brille putzen. Oder ein Kamera-Objektiv.

M. Gütiger Himmel! Aber warum haben Sie das nur gekauft, Beryl? Sie tragen doch nicht einmal eine Brille!

B. Ich trage Sonnenbrillen, und die werden hier in London schnell sehr schmutzig.

P. Aber warum haben Sie diese Flüssigkeit gekauft? Das würde ich gerne wissen.

B. Der junge Mann **hat sein Produkt sehr gut angepriesen. Er hat ein**

very good case for buying the stuff.

P. How?

B. First of all, he **caught my attention** with a friendly smile and he approached me in a way where I didn't feel under pressure. He asked me if he could **demonstrate the effectiveness** of the liquid and I gave him my sunglasses. The cleaning fluid made a real difference. Then he **persuaded** me that it was worth using the liquid because the lenses of the sunglasses were expensive and should be treated well. He **made a very sensible and persuasive case for buying** his product.

P. And there you see a successful salesperson at work ...

sehr gutes Argument dafür angebracht, dieses Zeug **zu kaufen**.

P. Und wie?

B. Zunächst mal **hat** er **meine Aufmerksamkeit** mit einem freundlichen Lächeln **erregt** und er hat sich mir in einer Weise genähert, durch die ich mich nicht bedrängt fühlte. Er hat mich gefragt, ob er mir **die Wirksamkeit** der Flüssigkeit **vorführen** dürfte und ich habe ihm meine Brille gegeben. Die Reinigungsflüssigkeit hat wirklich gut gewirkt. Dann **überzeugte** er mich davon, dass es sich lohnen würde, die Flüssigkeit zu benutzen, da Sonnenbrillengläser teuer wären und gut gepflegt werden sollten. Er **hat sehr vernünftige und überzeugende Verkaufsargumente vorgebracht**.

P. Und da sieht man einen guten Verkäufer bei der Arbeit ...

Background Information

Beryl says that the salesman in Leicester Square **made a very good sales pitch and made out a very good case for buying** the lens-cleaning liquid.
We looked at the meaning of to make »a sales pitch« in the last section; »to make out a case for something« has a similiar meaning like »to make a sales pitch«, i.e. to argue in favour of something in order to persuade the other person. e.g. »He made a great case for including Jonathon on our new sales seminars.«

> Other phrases with »**make**« include:
>
> | | |
> |---|---|
> | to make headway | to make progress |
> | to make allowances for | to prepare for the possibility of someone/something in future plans |
> | to make a bid for | to make an effort (usually financial) in order to achieve something |
> | to make an impact | to make a strong impression |
> | to make a point of | to do always something, or to take particular care in doing something |
> | to make amends for | to correct a past mistake |
> | to make a stand on | to unite in favour of something |

 **Train Yourself**

Verwenden Sie die oben stehenden Wendungen in den folgenden Sätzen!

1. The managing director ▓▓▓▓▓▓▓▓▓▓ congratulating the sales staff for the new orders received from Japan.
2. The success of the new advertising campaign was responsible for ▓▓▓▓▓▓▓▓▓▓ into the virgin market.
3. The company ▓▓▓▓▓▓▓▓▓▓ takeover ▓▓▓▓▓▓▓▓▓▓ for Watsons Pharmaceuticals.
4. Susan ▓▓▓▓▓▓▓▓▓▓ for losing the last order by increasing her sales ratio by 20 per cent.
5. When dealing with overseas customers one must ▓▓▓▓▓▓▓▓▓▓ for different customs and tastes.
6. In order to ▓▓▓▓▓▓▓▓▓▓ successful ▓▓▓▓▓▓▓▓▓▓ one must have total belief in the product and in oneself.
7. The administrative personnel in the company ▓▓▓▓▓▓▓▓▓▓ on increased overtime and more flexible working hours.
8. At their meeting Rupert ▓▓▓▓▓▓▓▓▓▓ increased investment in the Eastern European market.
9. Michael's personal touch really ▓▓▓▓▓▓▓▓▓▓! The deal was agreed and signed within hours!

 **Talk Talk Talk**

(Chip, the courier, enters office)

M. Hello, Chip! You're just in time to take part in our own **sales seminar**.

C. Seminar. What's that?

M. We'd like to ask you a couple of questions to support some theories we are developing.

C. Look, the only theory I want developed right now is the correct address for this packet Lucy gave me. I've biked halfway across London and there's no company at this address.

L. Give it to me, Chip. I'll **sort** this **out** for you ...

M. And in the meantime you can answer some of our questions. For instance, when did you last buy anything from a salesperson, without actually choosing the item yourself?

C. I bought a few apples from a **barrow** in Shaftesbury Avenue this

(Chip, der Kurier, betritt das Büro)

M. Hallo, Chip! Du kommst gerade rechtzeitig, um an unserem privaten **Verkaufsseminar** teilzunehmen.

C. Ein Seminar? Was läuft da ab?

M. Wir würden dir gerne ein paar Fragen stellen, um ein paar Theorien zu bestätigen, die wir gerade aufstellen.

C. Also hören Sie, die einzige Theorie, die ich gerade bestätigt haben möchte ist die korrekte Adresse für dieses Paket, das Lucy mir gegeben hat. Ich bin mit dem Motorrad durch halb London gefahren, aber es gibt keine Firma an dieser Adresse.

L. Gib es mir, Chip. Ich **kläre** das für dich ...

M. Und in der Zwischenzeit kannst du ein paar unserer Fragen beantworten. Wann hast du zum Beispiel das letzte Mal etwas von einem Verkäufer gekauft, ohne dir das Produkt selbst ausgesucht zu haben?

C. Ich habe heute Morgen ein paar Äpfel von einem **Straßenstand** auf

morning, if that's what you're looking for. Anyone like one?

M. Thanks, Chip. Now that's interesting. Why did you buy the apples? Did you suddenly have the urge to eat an apple? Did you go looking for apples?

C. No, not exactly. This barrowboy was shouting out »apples, fresh from the farm«, and I suddenly thought I'd like to sink my teeth into one.

P. And there you have it! Another example of **good salesmanship**. And you've sold me on those apples, Chip. Can I take you up on your offer of one?

C. Help yourself, Mr Brückner. They really are good.

der Shaftesbury Avenue gekauft, wenn Sie das meinen. Möchte jemand einen?

M. Danke, Chip. Das ist ja interessant. Warum hast du diese Äpfel gekauft? Hattest du plötzlich Heißhunger auf einen Apfel? Bist du auf der Suche nach Äpfeln gewesen?

C. Nein, nicht ganz. Der Junge am Stand rief »Äpfel, frisch vom Bauernhof«, und plötzlich hatte ich den Wunsch, in einen davon hineinzubeißen.

P. Da haben wir es! Ein weiteres Beispiel für **gute Verkaufskunst**. Und du hast mir diese Äpfel gut verkauft, Chip. Gilt dein Angebot noch?

C. Bedienen Sie sich, Mr Brückner. Sie sind wirklich gut.

 Train Yourself

»Let me, let him/her, let's, ...« – Schreiben Sie nachfolgende Sätze um, indem Sie »let« auf korrekte Weise in die Sätze einbauen.

1. Why don't we consider offering this new product for sale?

....
....

2. I'd just like to think the idea over.

   ....
   ....

3. Come in, sit down and look over this proposal with me.

   ....

4. It's a fine day - get out the car and join me for a drive into the mountains.

   ....
   ....

5. She should fax this cost analysis to the customer right away.

   ....
   ....

6. The company will just have to wait another week for delivery – they are always so impatient.

   ....
   ....

7. Allow me to explain what we have in mind.

   ....
   ....

8. Why don't we join in this new venture?

   ....
   ....

Talk Talk Talk

(Steve Blackman arrives at office)

S. Hello, hello, hello! This is quite a **confab**. **What's on the agenda**?

M. We're treading on your territory, Steve - we're discussing what makes a good salesperson.

(Steve Blackman betritt das Büro)

S. Aber hallo! Hier findet ja eine richtige **Konferenz** statt. **Was steht denn auf der Tagesordnung?**

M. Wir dringen gerade in dein Gebiet ein, Steve – wir diskutieren darüber, was einen guten Verkaufsmitarbeiter auszeichnet.

S. You're looking at him right now, Melissa!

M. Modesty is not your strong point, is it Steve?

S. **Modesty is perhaps the last quality a good salesperson needs**. You have to think constantly **in terms of the best** – and that means thinking you're the best, too. Or at least, better than the opposition.

M. You'll get your chance to demonstrate that at that seminar you and Peter are attending.

S. My God, I'd quite forgotten that – it's next week, isn't it?

M. Don't worry. I know Lucy has made all the preparations for you, isn't that right, Lucy?

L. Yes – **hotel rooms are booked, train tickets are on my desk**, together with **details of your hire car** for the trip to Scotland. All you have to do is pack.

S. Sie haben gerade einen vor sich, Melissa!

M. Bescheidenheit ist nicht gerade Ihre Stärke, was, Steve?

S. **Bescheidenheit ist vielleicht die letzte Eigenschaft, die ein guter Verkäufer braucht.** Sie müssen ständig immer nur **in den Kategorien des Besten** denken – und das bedeutet auch, dass man sich selbst für den Besten halten muss. Oder zumindest, dass man besser ist als die Gegenseite.

M. Sie werden die Chance haben, das auf dem Seminar zu beweisen, an dem Peter und Sie teilnehmen.

S. Mein Gott, das hätte ich fast vergessen – es findet nächste Woche statt, oder?

M. Keine Sorge. Ich weiß, dass Lucy alle Vorbereitungen für Sie getroffen hat, stimmt's, Lucy?

L. Ja - **die Hotelzimmer sind gebucht und die Bahnfahrkarten liegen auf meinem Schreibtisch**, zusammen mit den **Details Ihres Mietwagens** für die Fahrt nach Schottland. Alles, was Sie noch tun müssen, ist Koffer packen.

Background Information

While discussing what makes a good salesperson, Steve and Melissa use the comparative form »**better**« and the superlative form »**the best**«. English language learners at this level will be more than familiar with the general rules regarding comparatives and superlatives, i.e. adding »**-er/the -est**« to short adjectives and »**more/the most**« to longer ones, e.g. **shorter – the shortest, more beautiful – the most beautiful**. »**Better**« and »**the best**« are irregular, as is »**bad – worse – the worst**« and »**far – further**« (or »**farther**«) – »**the furthest**« (»**the farthest**«), the remainder following the general rule.

Train Yourself

Untenstehend finden Sie nun durcheinandergeratene Sätze, die solche Komparativ/Superlativ-Konstruktionen enthalten. **Bringen Sie sie in die richtige Reihenfolge!**

Beispiel: by this the memory living worst is disaster in far
This is by far the worst disaster in living memory.

1. practice on significantly more than was it more the attractive paper was in it

....
....

2. our is sales our office marketing nowhere big as near as office

....
....

3. most business the I seen is comprehensive far this journal by ever have

....
....

4. won the unquestionably Jones the account was ever most company had lucrative the

....
....

5. remain lower expected share little than a prices

6. diligent salesperson she the company was easily in most the

7. the trademark Marlboro world unquestionably is recognised in the most

8. much than sales the better previous informed is incumbent director present the

9. really serious expected had it not as was as we

 Vocabulary

brand	Marke
to catch s.o.'s attention	jds. Aufmerksamkeit erregen
confab	Geplauder/eine »Expertenrunde« (umgangssprachlich)
to demonstrate the effectiveness	die Wirksamkeit vorführen
to drop	hier: fallen lassen (eine Tätigkeit stehen und liegen lassen/ auch: eine Bemerkung fallen lassen etc.)
to fall for	sich verlieben
to fill in	über etwas aufklären/ ins Bild setzen
to follow up	folgen lassen/auch: Verfolgung
further afield	weiter weg
to gather	hier: gehört haben

to gear up	in Erwartung/voll ausgestattet sein
guinea-pig	Meerschweinchen, oft im Sinne von »Versuchskaninchen«
to hand out	ausgeben, verteilen
It has got a buzz	etwas brummt (vor Besuchern)/ hat Pep
to immerse oneself	sich in etwas versenken; intensiv vertraut machen
to make out a very good case	ein sehr gutes Argument dafür
packaging	Verpackung
run down	erschöpft, hier: schlecht gemacht
salesmanship	Verkaufsgeschäft; Verkaufen
salesperson	Verkaufspersonal
sales operation	Tagesaktivitäten
sales pitch	Verkaufsargument; Verkaufsstrategie
sales points	Verkaufsstellen
sales representative	Verkäufer
sales stand	Verkaufsstand
sales trip	Verkaufsreise
schedule	Terminkalender
sloppy	schlampig, nachlässig
to sort out	klassifizieren, einteilen
to sort out sth. for sb.	für jdn. etw. erklären
What's on the agenda?	Was steht auf der Tagesordnung
When it comes to selling ...	Wenn es darum geht ... anzupreisen
wild about	wild/verrückt nach

Demonstrate products
Produkte präsentieren

 **Here we go**

Peter hat seine ersten Schritte in der Verkaufsabteilung hinter sich gebracht und soll nunmehr sein Wissen und Verkaufsgeschick weiter vertiefen, indem er mit seinem Kollegen Steve Blackman auf ein Verkaufsseminar geschickt wird. Die Reisevorbereitungen sind bereits getroffen und Peter und Steve machen sich auf den Weg nach Bournemouth, wo das Seminar stattfinden soll. Peter ist gespannt, ob seine Fähigkeiten dieser Bewährungsprobe standhalten und hofft, sich weitere nützliche Kenntnisse aneignen zu können ...

 Talk Talk Talk

(Waterloo Station, London. Steve and Peter meet)

S. Hello there, Peter! You're **right on time**. We've got time for a coffee before the train goes.

P. Great! I didn't really **have time** for breakfast this morning.

S. Then come on. I'm buying ...

(In the train)

S. You certainly brought a lot of luggage, Peter.

(Waterloo Station, London. Steve und Peter treffen sich)

S. Hallo Peter! Sie kommen **gerade rechtzeitig**. Wir haben noch Zeit für einen Kaffee, bevor der Zug losfährt.

P. Toll! Ich **hatte** heute Morgen überhaupt keine **Zeit**, richtig zu frühstücken.

S. Dann kommen Sie. Ich zahle...

(Im Zug)

S. Peter, Sie haben aber eine Menge Gepäck dabei.

P. If we are away for two weeks I'll need it all. And I've got all my books with me.

P. Wenn wir zwei Wochen unterwegs sind, brauche ich das alles. Und ich habe alle meine Bücher dabei.

S. German books?

S. Deutsche Bücher?

P. Some, but mostly ones I picked up in London. I want to understand what's going on, so I did a bit of preparation.

P. Einige davon, aber die meisten habe ich aus London mitgenommen. Ich will genau wissen, was los ist, deshalb habe ich mich ein bisschen vorbereitet.

S. You'll have no difficulty. **I know the scene**, so stick with me.

S. Sie werden keine Schwierigkeiten haben, **ich kenne mich aus**, also halten Sie sich an mich.

P. Don't worry, Steve. I won't leave your side. You're the expert …

P. Keine Sorge, Steve. Ich werde nicht von Ihrer Seite weichen. Sie sind der Experte …

Background Information

Steve tells Peter that he's **right on time** and that they **have time** for a coffee before the train leaves. Peter is pleased because he didn't really have time for breakfast that morning.
»To **have time** for something« clearly means that the action can be carried out without being the participant being late, i.e. the coffee can be drunk and the train will still be there.
»To **be on time**« means to be somewhere at the precise time arranged. Contrast this with »**in time**«, meaning to be somewhere before or at the period of time arranged. e.g. The seminar starts at 8 o'clock. Peter is on time. He gets there at 8 o'clock exactly. Steve gets there at 7.50. He's in time for the seminar.

There are many other expressions with the word »**time**«. Some of them are listed below:

to kill time	to do something to pass the time
from time to time	sometimes, now and then
to pass the time of day	to meet someone you know and then talk about general or unimportant things, e.g. the weather
about time	when something is finally done which the speaker feels should have been done earlier
in the nick of time	at the last possible moment
for the time being	for the present; until the situation changes
to take one's time	not to hurry, to be slow and careful

 Train Yourself

In fünf der folgenden Sätze verbergen sich Fehler. **Finden Sie sie und schreiben Sie dann die fehlerhaften Sätze in korrekter Form!**

1. We got there just for the time being. The train was just leaving.

2. The situation in the Japanese stock market seems healthy for the time being but who knows what will happen in the future?

3. About time the managing director pays us a visit to make sure everything is running smoothly.

4. We got there just to kill time! The meeting was just starting.

5. It's from time to time they fixed that photocopier! It's been playing havoc for ages!

6. It's important in sales to pass the time of day with a client before going for the hard sell.

7. The summer holiday period is always a slow time for the company. People have nothing to do and just sit around in the nick of time.

8. Every year I have to give a small speech at the company dinner. I always try to relax and take my time over my words but I still get nervous.

9. It's very important to be in the nick of time when meeting a client. It creates a very bad impression if one is late.

10. OK, do we have time for a final rundown of tomorrow's events?

Colloquial English

stick with me	stay with me
to get hold of the wrong end of the stick	to misunderstand something
a stick-in-the-mud	an unadventurous person who refuses to do anything unusual

 **Talk Talk Talk**

(Steve and Peter arrive at their hotel)

(Steve und Peter kommen in ihrem Hotel an)

S. Good evening. We have **booked two rooms under the names** Blackman and Brückner. Our office called last week to make the booking.

S. Guten Abend. Wir haben **zwei Zimmer auf die Namen** Blackman und Brückner **gebucht**. Unser Büro hat die **Reservierung** letzte Woche telefonisch vorgenommen.

(Hotel receptionist) Yes, here we are. Two single rooms. You're here for the seminar?

(Hotelangestellter an der Rezeption) Ja, da haben wir es. Zwei Einzelzimmer. Sind Sie wegen des Seminars hier?

S. Yes, we're from ERGO Limited.

S. Ja, wir sind von ERGO Limited.

(Receptionist) There's a **reception** in the lounge at six for participants.

S. **That's just the ticket.** I need a drink after that journey. In fact, Peter, let's have a quickie in the bar before settling into our rooms.

P. **My treat!** What will it be?

S. A double Scotch for me. What about you?

P. I'm so thirsty I'm going to have a beer. Are we having dinner here?

S. The **seminar programme includes** all meals, but if the food is no good we can always eat out.

(Hotelangestellter an der Rezeption) Es gibt für die Teilnehmer um sechs Uhr ein **Treffen** in der Lounge.

S. **Das ist genau das Richtige.** Nach dieser Reise brauche ich einen Drink. Peter, lassen Sie uns einen kurzen Drink an der Bar nehmen, bevor wir auf unsere Zimmer gehen.

P. **Das geht auf meine Rechnung!** Was darf's sein?

S. Für mich einen doppelten Scotch. Und für Sie?

P. Ich habe solchen Durst, ich nehme ein Bier. Essen wir hier zu Abend?

S. Im **Seminarprogramm sind** alle Speisen **inbegriffen**, aber sollte das Essen nicht gut sein, können wir immer noch auswärts essen.

False Friends

»**Receptionist**« and »**reception**« have the same root verb – to receive – but there similarity ends. A receptionist »**receives**« or welcomes guests at a hotel, patients at the doctor's or dentist's surgery, visitors to an office. A reception, in the normal sense, is an »**Empfang**«.

There are several words/expressions in English that come from the root word »to receive«, apart from »**reception**« and »**receptionist**«:

receptive	an adjective describing somebody who is quick or willing to receive new ideas

a recipient	a person who receives something.
a receiver	an official appointed by law to look after the property of a bankrupt
in receivership	to be under control of an Official Receiver
to receive (somebody)	to welcome guests (formal)
to be on the receiving end of (something)	to suffer something unpleasant
to reciprocate	to do something in return for something
in receipt of something	having received something (usually a letter - formal)

 **Train Yourself**

Füllen Sie die Lücken mit oben stehenden Begriffen!

1. We are ▬▬▬▬ your letter of March 13th concerning the proposed takeover …
2. The company has gone ▬▬▬▬ after a disastrous slump in profits.
3. We were ▬▬▬▬ by the ambassador in his private office.
4. We would like ▬▬▬▬ the loyalty shown us by our clients by offering a new special offer.
5. There were nearly 50,000 ▬▬▬▬ last year of our advertising circular.
6. The ▬▬▬▬ was held in the hotel lounge.
7. I don't think the marketing director was very ▬▬▬▬ to our ideas.
8. Have you met our new ▬▬▬▬, Mrs Peters?
9. One of our clerical staff was ▬▬▬▬ a tongue – lashing from the sales director after mislaying an important document.
10. We had to call in the ▬▬▬▬ after the company was declared bankrupt.

 **Talk Talk Talk**

(At the reception, John Barlowe, who will **conduct the seminar**, welcomes Steve and Peter)

J. How do you do, I'm John Barlowe. I'll be conducting the seminar, so we'll be seeing quite a bit of each other in the next few days. Now, what are you having to drink?

S. That's very kind of you. I'm Steve Blackman, by the way, **Sales Director** of ERGO Limited, and this is our **Assistant Managing Director**, Peter Brückner, from Germany.

J. Germany? I've conducted a few seminars there. In English – for companies selling to Britain or the United States or looking for **market openings** there.
Very interesting they were, too.

P. I'm doing it the other way, by coming to England and getting **first-hand experience** with a company here.

J. Probably the **best way of going about it**, too. Do you have **sales experience**?

(Am Empfang, John Barlowe, der **das Seminar leiten** wird, begrüßt Steve und Peter)

J. Wie geht es Ihnen? Ich bin John Barlowe. Ich werde das Seminar leiten, also werden wir uns in den nächsten Tagen wohl ziemlich oft sehen. Also, was möchten Sie trinken?

S. Das ist sehr nett von Ihnen! Ich bin übrigens Steve Blackman, **Verkaufsleiter** von ERGO Limited, und das ist Peter Brückner, unser **stellvertretender Geschäftsführer** aus Deutschland.

J. Deutschland? Ich habe dort ein paar Seminare abgehalten. Auf Englisch – da die Unternehmen Verkaufskontakte in England oder in den Vereinigten Staaten haben oder dort nach **Markteröffnungen** suchen.
Sie waren auch sehr interessant.

P. Ich mache das genau andersherum, indem ich nach England gekommen bin und hier **eigene Erfahrungen** mit einem Unternehmen **sammle**.

J. Das ist wahrscheinlich auch **der beste Weg, die Sache anzugehen**. Haben Sie **Erfahrungen im Verkauf**?

P. Only what I've learnt from Steve here, during a **secondment** to his department. The idea is for me to immerse myself totally in each **area of the business**. Sales is where I am now.

J. I don't know if what I have to offer is really necessary for your work, but you'll find it interesting, I'm sure. I'll see you both at 9 AM sharp tomorrow, then. Enjoy the evening!

P. Nur das, was ich von Steve hier gelernt habe, während ich seiner Abteilung **unterstellt war**. Die Idee dahinter ist es, mich in jedes **Geschäftsgebiet** einzuarbeiten. Momentan bin ich im Verkauf.

J. Ich weiß nicht, ob das was ich Ihnen anzubieten habe, für Ihre Arbeit wirklich notwendig ist, aber Sie werden es sicherlich interessant finden. Ich sehe Sie also beide morgen pünktlich um 9 Uhr vormittags. Genießen Sie den Abend!

Background Information

John Barlowe in this section of Talk Talk Talk, referring to Peter's methods of gaining business experience, says that **he's going about it in the right way.** »To go about doing something« means **the approach or the way in which something is done**. Other »go«-expressions include:

to go hand in hand	to be connected or closely related
touch and go	a very risky or uncertain situation
to let oneself go	to enjoy oneself in a free and natural manner
to go it alone	to do something without anyone's help
from the word go	from the beginning
to go all out	to attempt to do something with the greatest possible determination
to go over with a fine toothcomb	to check very carefully for mistakes
to go without saying	to be understood and agreed without needing to be mentioned or proved
to make a go of something	to make a success of something

 **Train Yourself**

Verwenden Sie diese Wendungen in den folgenden Sätzen!

1. Right, George, I want you to ▓▓▓▓▓▓▓▓ this report ▓▓▓▓▓▓▓▓ and make sure there are no inaccuracies.
2. Everybody in the company ▓▓▓▓▓▓▓▓ to ensure the success of the new account.
3. It ▓▓▓▓▓▓▓▓ that a successful salesperson must believe in himself and in the product he is selling.
4. I really want to ▓▓▓▓▓▓▓▓ this. If it's a success we'll all reap the benefits.
5. After a brief training period the new salesperson was allowed to ▓▓▓▓▓▓▓▓ .
6. It was ▓▓▓▓▓▓▓▓ whether the new proposals would be accepted.
7. Helen ▓▓▓▓▓▓▓▓ the job in a very unprofessional manner resulting in her contract being terminated.
8. The marketing campaign for Rise and Shine breakfast cereal was doomed to failure ▓▓▓▓▓▓▓▓ . Consumer response was very disappointing.
9. At the office party everybody ▓▓▓▓▓▓▓▓ and there were some red faces next morning!
10. Belief in a product, the sufficient energy involved to sell it and good promotions work all ▓▓▓▓▓▓▓▓ in creating an effective salesperson.

 **Talk Talk Talk**

(John Barlowe welcomes participants at start of seminar)

J. I'd like to welcome you all to this **seminar on salesmanship**. I'm sure that at least I will enjoy it and also learn something from it. Salesmanship is an open-ended

(John Barlowe begrüßt am Anfang des Seminars die Teilnehmer)

J. Ich begrüße Sie alle bei unserem **Verkaufsseminar.** Ich bin mir sicher, dass wenigstens ich es genießen und etwas daraus lernen werde. Im Bereich des Verkaufs

area of study. There's no set **agenda**. There are no rules. Some successful sales people say you can't learn how to sell successfully. So I won't be lecturing you on the subject. I'll just **throw in ideas** and hope that you will contribute yours. Then we'll try to find **consensus**. But I have some **preliminary observations** I have formed during these seminars, which I have been holding now for more than ten years. Basically I sum them up with the acronym **PEP**. That stands for **Product, Energy, Promotion**. If you lack one you lack them all. Without a product, of course, you have nothing to sell – that's obvious. But it has to be a product you believe in, something you know you can sell. But how do you sell it? That's where energy comes in. You can have the best product in the world, but unless you go vigorously about selling it it's not going to move from the **warehouse floor**. And **that's where promotion comes in**. You can talk all day about your product but unless your energy is matched by promotional material it's all wasted effort. When all three are working together you have a recipe for success. Now, any questions?

lernt man nie aus. Es gibt keine feste **Tagesordnung**. Es gibt keine Regeln. Einige erfolgreiche Leute aus dem Verkauf meinen, man könnte nicht lernen, erfolgreich zu verkaufen. Deshalb werde ich Sie in dieser Sache auch nicht unterrichten. Ich werde nur **Ideen einbringen** und hoffe, dass Sie ihrerseits weitere beisteuern. Dann werde ich versuchen, eine **Übereinstimmung** zu finden. Trotzdem habe ich in diesen Seminaren, die ich seit mittlerweile zehn Jahren abhalte, einige **grundlegende Feststellungen** definiert. Im Großen und Ganzen fasse ich sie mit dem Akronym **PEP** zusammen. Das steht für **Produkt, Energie, Promotion**. Wenn Ihnen eines davon fehlt, fehlen Ihnen alle. Natürlich haben Sie ohne ein Produkt nichts zu verkaufen – das ist offensichtlich. Aber es muss ein Produkt sein, an das Sie glauben - etwas, von dem Sie wissen, dass Sie es verkaufen können. Aber wie verkaufen Sie es? Hier kommt die Energie ins Spiel. Sie können das beste Produkt der Welt haben, aber wenn Sie sich nicht voller Energie daran machen, es zu verkaufen, wird es das **Lager** niemals verlassen. Und **an diesem Punkt kommt die Promotion ins Spiel**. Sie können den ganzen Tag über Ihr Produkt sprechen, aber so lange Ihre Energie nicht mit

	Promotionmaterial einhergeht, ist alles vergebene Mühe. Wenn alle drei Elemente kombiniert werden, haben Sie ein Erfolgsrezept. Nun, irgend welche Fragen?
(A participant poses a question)	(Ein Teilnehmer stellt eine Frage)
P. In my time, I've actually been called upon to sell products I did not at all believe in, or at the very least didn't particularly interest me. But the **commission basis** was high, or the contract a particularly attractive one.	P. Zu meiner Zeit wurde ich dazu aufgefordert, Produkte zu verkaufen, an die ich überhaupt nicht glaubte oder die mich zumindest nicht besonders interessierten. Aber die **Provisionsrate** war hoch oder der Vertrag besonders verlockend.
J. And did you sell successfully?	J. Und waren Sie erfolgreich im Verkauf?
P. To be quite honest, no!	P. Ehrlich gesagt, nein!
J. And there you have it! Your **lack of interest in your product** was certainly clear in your **sales approach**.	J. Da haben Sie es! Ihr **mangelndes Interesse an Ihrem Produkt** hat sich in Ihrem **Auftreten** sicherlich niedergeschlagen.
P. But how can I **overcome** that problem?	P. Aber wie kann ich dieses Problem **lösen**?
J. Get to know your product thoroughly. Nothing is that uninteresting. Look for all its attractive, **positive features** and emphasize those. And that brings me to another point: get to know your **competition**, your **competitors'**	J. Lernen Sie Ihr Produkt richtig kennen. Nichts ist völlig uninteressant. Suchen Sie all seine **attraktiven, positiven Seiten** und betonen Sie sie. Und das bringt mich auf einen anderen Punkt: Machen Sie sich mit Ihrer **Konkurrenz** ver-

products. **Seek out** all the advantages of your own product. That will certainly **kindle interest** in it and help you sell ...

traut, mit Ihren **Konkurrenzprodukten**. **Finden Sie** alle Vorteile Ihres eigenen Produktes **heraus**. Das wird sicherlich Ihr **Interesse** daran **entfachen** und Ihnen beim Verkauf helfen ...

Background Information

Peter is told in this section of the dialogue **to seek out the** advantages of his product in order to help him sell. »**To seek out something**« is **to look for and to find**. Other prepositional verbs in a similar context include:

to search for	to look for thoroughly
to look into	to investigate
to look someone up	to visit when in the area
to run over	to check
to sort out	to find a solution
to check up on somebody	to ascertain whether a person is behaving in a suitable way or not
to hunt down	to find somebody/something after a lot of effort
to come across	to find accidentally

Train Yourself

Verwenden Sie diese Wendungen in den folgenden Sätzen:

1. I was looking through my old files the other day and I ▮▮▮▮ this letter from Bob Stevens detailing the Adams account. What luck!
2. Management are ▮▮▮▮ the problem but as yet don't seem to be any closer to finding a solution.
3. I don't think it's necessary for Tom to ▮▮▮▮ us. We're quite capable of doing the job on our own.
4. Don't forget to ▮▮▮▮ me ▮▮▮▮ the next time you're in New York!
5. Steve, I've got that presentation to do tomorrow, I don't suppose you'd mind ▮▮▮▮ it with me, would you?

6. I'm exhausted! I finally managed to ▬▬▬▬▬ that old client of ours! I've been trying all day! He must have moved houses five times!
7. There's something wrong with the printer, can you ▬▬▬▬ it ▬▬▬▬ ?
8. I've been ▬▬▬▬▬ that invoice all day and I still can't find it!
9. We need to ▬▬▬▬▬ new business opportunities to increase our share of the market.

 Talk Talk Talk

J. I hope you all enjoyed your lunch. Now we're going to play a little game I've made up. Divide yourselves up into groups of two please.

S. I'll stay with you Peter, if you don't mind.

J. I'm going to distribute these **envelopes**. In each one is the description of a product which our group - your company - has to sell. You'll have the afternoon to work out a **sales strategy** and tomorrow morning I want each group **to put its case**. Then we'll take a democratic vote to discover the most successful team, the company that is selling its product the best.

S. Here you are Peter. Open it up. What have we got to sell?

J. Ich hoffe, Sie haben Ihr Mittagessen genossen. Wir werden jetzt ein kleines Spiel spielen, das ich mir ausgedacht habe. Teilen Sie sich bitte in Zweiergruppen auf.

S. Peter, ich bleibe bei Ihnen, wenn Sie nichts dagegen haben.

J. Ich werde nun diese **Umschläge** verteilen. In jedem befindet sich die Beschreibung eines Produktes, das Ihre Gruppe - Ihr Unternehmen - verkaufen muss. Sie haben den Nachmittag über Zeit, eine **Verkaufsstrategie** auszuarbeiten und morgen früh möchte ich, dass jede Gruppe **Ihren Fall vorträgt**. Dann werden wir über das erfolgreichste Team abstimmen, über das Unternehmen, das sein Produkt am besten verkauft.

S. Hier bitte, Peter. Öffnen Sie es. Was müssen wir verkaufen?

P. It's a new kind of vacuum cleaner, as far as I can make out.

P. Es ist eine neue Art Staubsauger, so weit ich das beurteilen kann.

S. Oh, just the ticket! From **high-tech** to home-care. We've taken a big step back.

S. Na, genau das Richtige! Von der **Hochtechnologie** zur Hauspflege! Wir haben einen großen Schritt zurück gemacht.

P. I think the point of this vacuum-cleaner is that it is a high-tech product. But we'll need some time to study the **specifications** and all this literature on it.

P. Ich glaube, das Interessante an diesem Staubsauger ist, dass er ein hochmodernes Produkt ist. Aber wir werden ein bisschen Zeit brauchen, um die **näheren Angaben** und die entsprechende Literatur zu studieren.

S. I know just the place. I've discovered a very cosy bar just down the road. Let's take up a corner table there and **get down to work**!

S. Dafür kenne ich den idealen Ort. Ich habe die Straße herunter eine sehr nette Bar entdeckt. Setzen wir uns dort an einen Ecktisch und **fangen mit der Arbeit an**!

Background Information

Steve knows a nice cosy bar **to get down to work** for their sales strategy. This means **to begin seriously to deal with something**. Here are a few more phrasal verbs with the word »**down**«:

to back down	to yield in an argument
to put something down to	to explain the cause of
to come down on	to punish or blame someone for something
to bring down	to cause to become less
to stand down	to give up one's official position
to lay down	to state a rule (especially »lay down the law«)
to come down to	to be in the end a matter of

Train Yourself

Schreiben Sie die folgenden Sätze noch einmal und ersetzen Sie dabei die hervorgehobenen Wörter durch oben stehende Wendungen.

1. The Managing Director *is retiring* at the end of the year.

2. – I wonder why the sales figures this year are so low?
   – Personally, I *blame* the recession.

3. At the end of the day the success of a company all *depends on* the degree of efficiency in which it is run.

4. When a new manager takes over a company he must *enforce* the law to ensure that things run the way he wants them to.

5. If everybody refused to *compromise* during negotiations no deal would ever be reached.

6. (At the meeting) – Good morning everybody. Now I think we all know each other so let's *start* doing business.

7. – I think we should *reduce* the price in order to make it more cost-effective. Prices are too high for the consumer right now.

8. The Advertising Standards Council promised *to severely punish* any companies using underhand methods to sell their products.

Talk Talk Talk

(Next morning at the seminar) (Am nächsten Morgen beim Seminar)

J. Good morning, ladies and gentlemen! I hope you slept well and are prepared for a productive

J. Guten Morgen, meine Damen und Herren! Ich hoffe, Sie haben gut geschlafen und sind bereit für

morning. Let's get down to business. Mr Blackman and Mr Brückner - let's hear your **presentation** first.

S. We start from the assumption that because there are so many **brands and types** of vacuum cleaner on the market we have to persuade **potential agents and clients** that **it really is worth their while investing** in ours. Now how do we do that ? Over to you, Peter!

P. With a product such as a vacuum cleaner we have to start at the level of the agent, **persuading** him or her **to carry our range**. The days of the door-to-door salesman are really over – at least, in Germany! We believe that our product, because of its **advanced technology**, using centrifugal force, offers a distinct break from conventional, increasingly old-fashioned models. It is cleaner, **more efficient and cost-effective**. For a start, there is no longer any need to use dust-bags, a huge advantage for the busy housewife – or, as we say in German, Hausmann!

einen produktiven Morgen. Kommen wir gleich zur Sache. Mr. Blackman und Mr. Brückner – lassen Sie uns als Erstes Ihre **Präsentation** hören.

S. Wir beginnen mit der Annahme, dass wir, weil es so viele **Marken und Arten** von Staubsaugern auf dem Markt gibt, die **potenziellen Vertreter und Kunden** davon überzeugen müssen, **dass unserer wirklich sein Geld wert ist**. Nun, wie machen wir das? Ich übergebe an Peter!

P. Mit einem Produkt wie dem Staubsauger müssen wir auf der Ebene des Vertreters anfangen – ihn oder sie davon **überzeugen, unser Sortiment zu übernehmen**. Die Tage des von Tür zu Tür gehenden Vertreters sind vorbei – wenigstens in Deutschland! Wir glauben, dass unser Produkt, da es eine **fortschrittliche Technologie** besitzt und auf Zentrifugalkraft basiert, einen klaren Bruch mit den konventionellen, langsam altmodisch werdenden Modellen anbietet. Es ist sauberer, **effizienter und kosteneffektiver**. Erst einmal brauchen wir keinen Staubsaugerbeutel mehr, ein großer Vorteil für die beschäftigte Hausfrau – oder den Hausmann, wie wir in Deutschland sagen!

S. We concentrate our **sales pitch** in three directions: **savings** in time and effort, particularly important in the case of a domestic appliance, new technology that is going to replace old-fashioned systems, and a competitive, economical price. Shall I go on?

J. Please do! I'm on the point of buying one of your machines ...

S. Wir konzentrieren uns mit unsere **Verkaufsstrategie** auf drei Richtungen: Einsparungen von Zeit und Energie, was bei Haushaltsgeräten besonders wichtig ist, neue Technologien, die altmodische Systeme ersetzen und ein konkurrenzfähiger, ökonomischer Preis. Soll ich fortfahren?

J. Ja, bitte! Ich bin fast so weit, Ihnen eine Ihrer Maschinen abzukaufen ...

Background Information

Peter and Steve begin their presentation by asking the question: »How do we persuade potential clients that it really **is worth their while investing** in our vacuum cleaner when there are so many others on the market?«

If something **is worth your while doing** then you **should follow out the advice** because you will benefit in some way (often financially) from your efforts. The word »**worth**« itself refers to the **value of something**; either to the amount of money something can be sold for (a painting is worth a million pounds etc.), or the importance or usefulness of something (a person is worth employing). A very common expression in English combines the two: »**She's worth her weight in gold.**«

Other expressions with **worth** include:

for all (your) worth	a great deal of effort
for what it's worth	an expression used when the person is unsure how useful or important a piece of information may be
to be not worth the paper something is printed on	to have very little value (a document)

worthless	having no value in money, being of no use
to make something worth someone's while	(colloquial) to pay somebody to do something
to be worth (your) salt	to be good at your job
worthy	a) deserving respect, admiration or support b) suitable for (e.g. »The dinner was worthy of a king«)

 **Train Yourself**

Vervollständigen Sie nun die unten stehenden Sätze mit diesen Wendungen! Manchmal passen mehrere Begriffe:

1. The new salesperson is really ▒▒▒▒▒▒▒▒▒▒! He's not stopped all morning!
2. I don't think it's ▒▒▒▒▒▒▒▒ our ▒▒▒▒▒▒▒▒ going over these figures again until we've both had a good night's rest. We're both exhausted.
3. What do you think of the new merger, Peter? Well, ▒▒▒▒▒▒▒▒, I don't think it's been thought out properly …
4. During my first year at the company I had to work ▒▒▒▒▒▒▒▒ my ▒▒▒▒▒▒▒▒ just to keep my head afloat.
5. The company invested a lot of time and effort in trying to find a ▒▒▒▒▒▒▒▒ successor to the outgoing sales director.
6. Julie, could you start earlier on the cleaning this week? We'll ▒▒▒▒▒▒▒▒.
7. This account is ▒▒▒▒▒▒▒▒. Sales figures for this quarter have been terrible.
8. There's a great danger of feeling ▒▒▒▒▒▒▒▒ after retirement from a company. One needs to remain active as much as possible.

 **Talk Talk Talk**

(Still at the seminar)

J. Right, let's hear the next team. Yes, fine, you two on my right ...

N. I'm Nigel Gibbs and this is my partner, Graham Cluver. Our job is to sell garden seeds. Unlike the company that preceded us, **our task is to market our product** using bright, promising **packaging and cataloguing**. Our products, basically seed packages, have to stand out and **attract attention** in the seed shops. We have to assume that our customers know what they are looking for and buy by sight. So our **sales approach** is to hire a good **marketing company** to design the packaging, the cover pictures and the catalogue.

G. I'd just like to add that planting instructions must be clearly written, and no **false promises** made. If we promise impossibly fast-growing and blooming sweet peas and they don't **match our claims** then

(Noch immer beim Seminar)

J. OK, lassen Sie uns das nächste Team hören. Ja gut, Sie beide zu meiner Rechten ...

N. Ich heiße Nigel Gibbs und das ist mein Partner Graham Cluver. Unsere Aufgabe besteht darin, Saatgut zu verkaufen. Im Gegensatz zu dem vorherigen Unternehmen **ist es unser Ziel, unser Produkt zu vermarkten**, indem wir glänzende, viel versprechende **Verpackung und Kataloge** verwenden. Unsere Produkte, in erster Linie Saatpackungen, müssen in Samenhandlungen ausgestellt werden und **Aufmerksamkeit erregen**. Wir müssen davon ausgehen, dass unsere Kunden wissen, was sie suchen und aufgrund ihrer Wahrnehmung kaufen. Deshalb besteht unsere **Verkaufsstrategie** darin, eine gute **Marketingfirma** damit zu beauftragen, die Verpackung, die Coverfotos und den Katalog zu entwerfen.

G. Ich möchte noch hinzufügen, dass die Pflanzanweisungen klar formuliert werden müssen und keine **falschen Versprechungen** gemacht werden dürfen. Wenn wir unglaublich schnell wachsende

we are working **counter-productively** and losing customers.

und ertragreiche Erbsen versprechen und **unsere Ansprüche** dann nicht **erfüllen**, arbeiten wir **kontraproduktiv** und verlieren unsere Kunden.

 **Train Yourself**

Bringen Sie die nachfolgenden Sätze ins Passiv!

Beispiel: Somebody delivered the parcel at 4 o'clock.
The parcel was delivered at 4 o'clock.

1. Somebody last saw John getting into a taxi.

2. Somebody published the report last year.

3. Somebody will announce the departure time later on today.

4. They make Fiat cars in Milan.

5. My secretary is typing out the work as we speak.

6. We have sold 10,000 units so far this month.

 Talk Talk Talk

(Steve and Peter are talking in the hotel lounge after dinner)

(Steve und Peter unterhalten sich nach dem Abendessen in der Hotel-Lounge)

S. Last day then tomorrow, Peter. Have you enjoyed it? More important, have you learnt much from the seminar?

S. Morgen ist also der letzte Tag, Peter. Hat es Ihnen Spaß gemacht? Oder noch wichtiger, haben Sie auf dem Seminar viel gelernt?

P. Yes, I think so. I like the interactive nature of it. **It matches the**

P. Ich glaube ja. Ich mag seinen interaktiven Charakter. **Er passt**

subject of the seminar perfectly. After all, what is selling if not **interactive**?

S. You're right there! But I'm still looking forward to getting on the road again, to Cardiff. We'll see a real **salesman** at work there. He's as Welsh as they come and he has a **natural ability for selling**. A natural asset, too – **the gift of the gab**!

(A seminar participant approaches)

B. Hello, I'm Barry Smythe – I hope I'm not intruding, but I would like to meet you and have a word with you.

S. Certainly. Sit down and join us.

B. That's very kind. Oddly enough I've just **won the franchise** to sell a revolutionary new vacuum-cleaner, made in Germany. I was most impressed by your presentation. I'm putting together a sales team now. You wouldn't be interested in joining it, would you? Or perhaps working for us **on a consultancy basis**? With your German background, Mr Brückner, you'd be invaluable.

perfekt zum Thema des Seminars. Außerdem, was ist Verkaufen – wenn nicht **interaktiv**?

S. Da haben Sie Recht! Aber ich freue mich schon darauf, wieder weiter zu fahren, nach Cardiff. Da werden wir einen richtigen **Vertreter** bei der Arbeit sehen. Er ist ein Waliser, wie Sie ihn sich nicht besser vorstellen können und er hat eine **natürliche Begabung fürs Verkaufen**. Und auch einen natürlichen Vorzug - **die Gabe einer großen Klappe**!

(Ein Seminarteilnehmer kommt)

B. Hallo, ich heiße Barry Smythe – ich hoffe, ich störe Sie nicht, aber ich wollte Sie gerne kennen lernen und mich mit Ihnen unterhalten.

S. Aber sicher. Setzen Sie sich zu uns.

B. Sehr nett. Seltsamerweise habe ich gerade **die Konzession** für den Verkauf eines revolutionären, neuen Staubsaugers »Made in Germany« **bekommen**. Ich war von Ihrer Präsentation sehr beeindruckt. Ich stelle gerade ein Verkaufsteam zusammen. Sie wären wohl nicht daran interessiert einzusteigen, nicht wahr? Oder **auf beratender Basis** für uns zu arbeiten? Mit Ihrem deutschen Hintergrund, Mr Brückner, wären Sie unbezahlbar.

S. (laughs) Vacuum-cleaners? **We're into computer software**, Mr Smythe. I found it difficult enough mastering that **business area**. Vacuum-cleaners are right **out of my league**. And Mr Brückner here is destined for much greater things. But thanks for the compliment, anyway. And good luck with that new vacuum-cleaner ...

S. (lacht) Staubsauger? **Wir arbeiten in der Software-Branche**, Mr. Smythe. Ich fand es schwierig genug, dieses **Geschäftsfeld** zu meistern. Staubsauger sind einfach **nicht mein Spezialgebiet**. Und Mr Brückner hier ist für Größeres bestimmt. Aber auf alle Fälle bedanken wir uns für das Kompliment. Und viel Glück mit dem neuen Staubsauger ...

Background Information

Peter says, »It matches the subject of the seminar **perfectly**«. »Perfectly«, as you know, is an adverb, the adjective is »perfect«. The opposite of »perfect« is »imperfect«.
Later, the adjectives »**real**« and »**natural**« are used. Their opposites are »unreal« and »unnatural«.

»**un-**« and »**in-**« are prefixes that are used to change the meaning of an adjective or adverb into an opposite one. For example: »important« – »unimportant«. Where a word begins with an »r« we generally use the prefix, »ir«, hence, regular – irregular and many words beginning in a vowel use »in« as in »inevitable« or »inarticulate«.

Train Yourself

Multiple Choice - Welches ist das richtige Präfix?
Geben Sie in den nachfolgenden Sätzen das Gegenteil an, indem Sie das richtige Präfix wählen:

1. It is (*im-/un-/in-*) _____ possible to get any work done with all this noise around me!

2. (*In-/im-/un-*) _____ fortunately the company lost the contract last year.

3. (*Ir-* /*un-*/*im-*) ▬▬▬▬▬▬▬▬ respective of the fact that the senior manager had a bad relationship with his staff, he also had difficulties with his superiors.

4. Julie would spend an (*un-*/*im-*/*ir-*) ▬▬▬▬▬▬▬▬ ordinate amount of time talking on the phone rather than getting her work done.

5. We were (*im-*/*un-*/*in-*) ▬▬▬▬▬▬▬▬ mobile for over half an hour the traffic was so bad.

6. I hadn't researched the subject of the meeting and so I felt very (*un-*/*im-*/*ir-*) ▬▬▬▬▬▬▬▬ comfortable throughout its duration.

7. The manager thought it was very (*un-*/*im-*/*ir-*) ▬▬▬▬▬▬▬▬ responsible of Peter to demand a pay-rise.

8. It was very (*un-*/*in-*/*im-*) ▬▬▬▬▬▬▬▬ usual for Harold to be late but this time was the exception to the rule.

9. It is (*in-*/*un-*/*im-*) ▬▬▬▬▬▬▬▬ acceptable for staff to wear (*in-*/*im-*/*un-*) ▬▬▬▬▬▬▬▬ appropriate clothes for work.

Vocabulary

advanced technology	fortschrittliche Technologie
agent	Vertreter
agenda	Tagesordnung
Assistant Managing Director	stellvertretender Geschäftsführer
to be out of s.o.'s league	Spezialgebiet von jdm. sein
to book	buchen
booking	Reservierung
brand	Marke
business area	Geschäftsgebiet, Geschäftsfeld
to carry s.o.'s range	jds. Sortiment übernehmen
client	Kunde
commission (basis)	Provisions(rate)
competition	Konkurrenz

competitors' products	Konkurrenzprodukte
consensus	Übereinstimmung, Konsens
cost-effective	kosteneffektiv
consultancy basis	beratende Funktion
counter-productive	kontraproduktiv
first-hand experience	eigene Erfahrungen
to get down to sth.	etw. angehen
to go about sth.	etw. angehen
to have time	Zeit haben
to kindle interest	Interesse entfachen
to know the scene	sich auskennen
to market	vermarkten
to match perfectly	perfekt passen
to match s.o.'s claim	jds. Ansprüche erfüllen
My treat!	Das geht auf meine Rechnung!
preliminary observations	grundlegende Feststellungen
promotional material	Promotionsmaterial
reception	Empfang
right on time	rechtzeitig
Sales Director	Verkaufsleiter
sales experience	Verkaufserfahrung
salesman	Vertreter
sales pitch/approach	Verkaufsstrategie
secondment	Abordnung, im Sinne von »jdm. unterstellt werden«
to seek out	finden, heraussuchen
seminar on salesmanship	Verkaufsseminar
specifications	nähere Angaben
task	Ziel
That's just the ticket.	Das ist genau das Richtige.
the gift of the gab	die Gabe einer großen Klappe
warehouse floor	Lager
to win the franchise	die Konzession bekommen

Make good deals
Geschäftsabschlüsse erzielen

 Here we go

Nach seinem Verkaufsseminar ist Peter nun bestens gewappnet für einen Ausflug in die Praxis. Er fährt mit Steve nach Cardiff und startet von dort aus Besuche in die Verkaufsvertretungen von ERGO Limited. Dort wird er mit den alltäglichen Aufgaben und Problemen von Außendienstmitarbeitern konfrontiert und versucht, so viel wie möglich über die eigentliche Verkaufstätigkeit zu lernen und auch seine eigenen Erfahrungen einzubringen …

 **Talk Talk Talk**

(Steve and Peter are on their way by train to Cardiff)

S. (sings softly) We're on the road again …

P. You like being **out and about**, Steve.

S. Love it, Peter, dear chap! I love the independence, the feeling that I'm my own man, out there in a world full of challenges. I envy my **salespeople** – I'd like to do more selling myself. But somebody has to look after the shop.

(Steve und Peter fahren mit dem Zug Richtung Cardiff)

S. (singt leise) Und weiter geht die Reise …

P. Sie sind wohl gern **unterwegs**, Steve.

S. Ich bin ganz versessen darauf, Peter, mein Bester! Ich liebe die Unabhängigkeit, das Gefühl, dass ich mein eigener Herr in einer Welt voller Herausforderungen bin. Ich beneide meine **Außendienstmitarbeiter** – ich würde gern viel öfter selbst auf Verkaufstour gehen. Aber irgendjemand muss ja dafür sorgen, dass der Laden läuft.

P. So tell me again what we can expect in Cardiff.

S. It's also a **one-man operation. Trevor does a good job** but he needs the occasional **check**, which we are doing. He has a **part-time sales force** and does reasonably good business. Wales is getting a lot of central government assistance, even though it has its own national assembly now. Some government departments moved to Wales in a decentralization process, and there's a lot of support for new small businesses. So there's **a lot of scope** for us there.

P. Dann erzählen Sie mir doch noch mal, was uns in Cardiff erwartet.

S. Ein **Ein-Mann-Betrieb**. Trevor **leistet gute Arbeit**, aber er braucht ab und zu einen **Kontrollbesuch**, und genau das tun wir. Er beschäftigt eine **Teilzeitkraft für den Verkauf** und das Geschäft läuft recht gut. Wales bekommt eine Menge Unterstützung von der Zentralregierung, auch wenn es jetzt seine eigene Nationalversammlung hat. Ein paar Dienststellen der Regierung sind im Rahmen eines Dezentralisierungsprogramms nach Wales gezogen und neue, kleine Betriebe werden kräftig unterstützt. Für uns gibt es dort also **ein breites Betätigungsfeld**.

Background Information

Steve tells Peter in this section of the dialogue that he loves being **out and about**, in other words **he likes to be outside**, travelling and meeting people, e.g. »I hate being stuck in this stuffy office, I'd rather be out and about«. There are several phrasal verbs with »**out and about**«:

to set about	to start working
to bring about	to cause to happen
to come about	to happen
to sort out	to find a solution
to bear out	to confirm the truth
to carry out	to complete a plan
to come out	to appear
to fall out with	to quarrel with somebody
to point out	to draw attention to the fact
to miss out on	to fail to get sth.

Train Yourself

Vervollständigen Sie nun die Sätze mit diesen Wendungen!

1. The problem was ▬▬▬ by Martin's resignation.
2. In the meeting it was ▬▬▬ that the deadline coincided with a national holiday.
3. The deal fell through and the managing director was anxious to know how this had ▬▬▬.
4. The quarterly prediction was ▬▬▬ by the eventual sales figures.
5. When the news ▬▬▬ everybody was in a state of disbelief.
6. Peter and Steve ▬▬▬ working as soon as they arrived at the hotel.
7. Now Susan, I don't want to ▬▬▬ with you but I'm not happy with your lack of punctuality.
8. We spent half the night trying to ▬▬▬ the discrepancy but still couldn't come to a solution.
9. Tom was very upset, it was the second time he had ▬▬▬ ▬▬▬ promotion.
10. The strategy was successfully ▬▬▬ and the new account was won.

 Talk Talk Talk

(Cardiff railway station)

S. We'll grab a taxi to the hotel and then **give** our man Trevor Jones **a call**. He can come round to the hotel for a drink or we would even invite him for a meal. What do you think?

(Im Bahnhof von Cardiff)

S. Wir schnappen uns ein Taxi zum Hotel und **rufen** unseren Trevor Jones dann **an**. Er kann dann auf einen Drink im Hotel vorbeikommen, wir könnten ihn sogar zum Essen einladen. Was halten Sie davon?

P. I'm easy. Perhaps it would be hospitable to invite him to join us for lunch, and at the same time we could get to know each other.

P. Mir ist das recht. Vielleicht wäre es ein Zeichen der Gastfreundschaft, ihn zum Mittagessen einzuladen und außerdem könnten wir uns dabei besser kennen lernen.

S. He's a nice fellow. I think you'll like him. An **easy-going** Welshman, but at the same time a good worker, a **good salesman** ... Here we are – the hotel. Let's get settled in first. I'll meet you in the bar in half an hour. And in the meantime I'll give Trevor a call ...

S. Er ist ein netter Kerl. Ich glaube, Sie werden ihn mögen. Er ist ein **unkomplizierter** Waliser, aber gleichzeitig ein guter Mitarbeiter und **Verkäufer** ... Da sind wir schon – das Hotel. Richten wir uns erst einmal ein. Wir treffen uns in einer halben Stunde in der Bar. Und in der Zwischenzeit rufe ich Trevor an ...

Background Information

On arrival at the hotel, Steve goes off to **give** Trevor **a call.** He could have said he was going to: **give** him **a ring, get on the phone** to him, or very colloquially, **give** him **a bell**.
Presuming Steve is ringing Trevor at his place of work, he may also need an extension number, to phone directly to his office or he might say, »Could you put me through to Trevor (surname)'s office please?«
»**To put somebody through to**« is **to connect** them with somebody.
If Trevor is **not available** the secretary or receptionist might reply: »I'm sorry/afraid he's **otherwise engaged**,« or »He's **being held** up in a meeting at the moment« or »He's **unavailable** at the moment«.

If Trevor is speaking on the phone to somebody else the receptionist might say: »I'm afraid his **line's busy** right now/at the moment, can I take a message?« or »Can you **hold the line**?«
Let's imagine Steve is able **to get through to** Trevor (to establish contact with him). This could be the beginning of their conversation:

- Hello is that Trevor Morris?
- Speaking.

- Hello Trevor, Steve Blackman here. How are you?
- Fine Steve. And you?
- Oh, not so bad. I'm just ringing to set up some things for tonight.
- Fine, fire away Steve.
- Well ...

»**Speaking**« in this context is used to confirm that the caller has got through to the right person; it is only used in telephone conversations. »**Fire away**« means to continue talking and is quite colloquial, used here because Steve and Trevor already know each other.

 Train Yourself

Sie sehen nun drei Ausschnitte aus Telefonaten. **Vervollständigen Sie sie mit den vorangegangenen Wendungen!**

1.
- Hello, this is Graham Brown here, can you (a) ▨▨▨▨▨▨ to Geoffrey Barclay, please?
- Certainly, (b) ▨▨▨▨▨▨, please. (A few seconds later) I'm (c) ▨▨▨▨▨▨ but he's ▨▨▨▨▨▨ in a meeting. Can I (d) ▨▨▨▨▨▨?
- Yes, can you tell him Geoffrey Barclay from ERGO Ltd called? He's got my number. I'll (e) ▨▨▨▨▨▨ later.
- Of course, Mr Barclay.
- Thank you.

2.
- Hello, I'd like to speak with Peter Lownes, please.
- (f) ▨▨▨▨▨▨.
- Oh, Hello Mr. Lownes. This is Steve Blackman from ERGO Ltd. I spoke to you last week. There's just some details I'd like to go over with you.
- Hello Mr. Blackman. I remember our conversation very well. Now, (g) ▨▨▨▨▨▨.

3.
- Good afternoon, ERGO Ltd. Can I help you?
- Yes, this Brenda Harte here from Heslop Communications, can I have

(h) ▓▓▓▓▓▓▓▓▓▓ 345, please?
- Certainly, one moment. (A few seconds later) Sorry, he's
(i) ▓▓▓▓▓▓▓▓▓▓ at the moment.
- Oh I see, well I'll try and (j) ▓▓▓▓▓▓▓▓▓▓ to him later. Thank you.

 **Talk Talk Talk**

(The hotel bar)

(In der Hotelbar)

S. You've unpacked already, Peter? What are you drinking?

S. Schon ausgepackt, Peter? Was möchten Sie trinken?

P. A pint of best bitter, please, Steve.

P. Ein Pint vom besten Bitter bitte, Steve.

S. Ah, here comes Trevor now! Hello, Trevor. Good to see you again. How's business? Oh, meet my colleague and our assistant managing director, Peter Brückner. He's from Germany and I'm **showing him the ropes** in the **sales area**.

S. Ah, da kommt Trevor ja! Hallo, Trevor. Schön, Sie wieder zu sehen. Wie läuft das Geschäft? Oh, darf ich Ihnen meinen Kollegen, unseren stellvertretenden Geschäftsführer Peter Brückner vorstellen? Er kommt aus Deutschland und ich **mache ihn mit den Grundzügen** des **Verkaufsbereiches vertraut**.

T. Pleased to meet you, Peter! How are you liking England?

T. Ich freue mich, Sie kennen zu lernen, Peter! Wie gefällt Ihnen England?

P. Loving it. Even the weather!

P. Ich liebe es. Selbst das Wetter!

T. You'll get to see some rough weather in the next couple of days. We have to **run up** to Swansea and a gale is forecast off the Atlantic.

T. In den nächsten Tagen werden Sie ein ziemlich stürmisches Wetter erleben. Wir werden hinauf nach Swansea müssen und es wurde ein Sturm über dem Atlantik vorhergesagt.

S. What will we be doing in Swansea?

T. There's a new **financial services company** up there and it's expressed interest in that new **financial exchange software. It will take some selling**, but it will help to have you two along. Makes us look a serious team.

S. Was werden wir denn in Swansea zu tun haben?

T. Es gibt da oben eine neue **Firma für Finanzdienstleistungen** und sie hat Interesse für dieses neue **Bilanzierungsprogramm** gezeigt. Es **wird einige harte Verkaufsgespräche geben**, aber es wird vielleicht nützlich sein, Sie beide dabei zu haben. Das wird uns den Eindruck eines ernsthaft bemühten Teams verleihen.

Background Information

Trevor says here that he has to **run up** to Swansea, in other words he has to drive there. »**Run up**« when used with the word »against« can also mean to encounter something, usually a problem, e.g. »The boss told me we had run up against a serious problem.«

Other phrases and expressions with »**run**« include:

to run over	to check something (also »run through« which has the the same meaning)
to run into	to meet somebody by chance
to run to	to have enough money for something
In the long run	after everything has been considered
to be in the running	to have a chance of winning something
to be run off one's feet	to be very busy
run-of-the-mill	ordinary or average
to run an eye over	to look quickly at something
to run its course	to continue to its natural end, to develop naturally

Train Yourself

Verwenden Sie diese Wendungen nun in der folgenden Übung!

1. The interviewees were so ▬▬▬▬▬▬▬ the director decided to re-advertise the position in order to seek out an exceptional candidate.
2. – I'm totally ▬▬▬▬▬▬▬! I haven't stopped all day!
3. – Hey, you'll never guess who I ▬▬▬▬▬▬▬ at that conference last weekend! Steve Jones!
4. The delegate ▬▬▬▬▬▬▬ final ▬▬▬▬▬▬▬ his notes and then began his speech.
5. The company decided against taking action and let the matter ▬▬▬▬▬▬▬.
6. Although the new software attracted a great deal of attention at its inception, sales were disappointing ▬▬▬▬▬▬▬.
7. Two new branches of the company were opened last year but due to high overheads, the shareholders felt they couldn't ▬▬▬▬▬▬▬ a third.
8. Two salespeople at ERGO Ltd are ▬▬▬▬▬▬▬ for the salesperson of the year award. They're both very excited.
9. (On the phone) – Oh hello John, Peter Davis here. Look, can we meet next week? We've ▬▬▬▬▬▬▬ some unforeseen difficulties with the Roberts account.
10. The itinerary for the day was ▬▬▬▬▬▬▬ several times before everybody was satisfied.

Talk Talk Talk

(The hotel lobby. Peter and Steve meet Trevor Jones)	(Die Lobby des Hotels. Peter und Steve treffen Trevor Jones)
S. Good morning, Trevor. You're bright and early.	S. Guten Morgen, Trevor. Sie sind ja ein echter Frühaufsteher.
T. The early bird catches the worm, **as they say in the trade**. But	T. Der frühe Vogel fängt den Wurm, **wie man in unserem Geschäft**

we're after more than worms, of course. The car is outside. We'll chat on the way to Swansea …

(During the journey)

T. Let me **fill you** both **in** on this job. This new software, Quickpay, is brand new and although it's revolutionary – perhaps precisely because it is so – it will take some selling at first. It attracted some attention in the **trade press** and I had a call from this Swansea company, LSD Financial Services. I sent them as much material on the system as I had – I want to talk to you about that Steve. It wasn't that good. Don't we have anything more? Something about the system's success in the States, perhaps?

S. I brought some new material with me. I haven't had a chance yet to give you it. It's an **up-to-date brochure**.

T. Great, that's just what I need. Now, let me explain our **strategy** in Swansea …

sagt. Aber wir sind natürlich hinter mehr her, als nur hinter ein paar Würmern. Das Auto steht draußen. Wir können auf dem Weg nach Swansea weiterreden …

(Während der Fahrt)

T. Ich werde **Sie** erst einmal über dieses Geschäft **ins Bild setzen**. Diese neue Software, Quickpay, ist brandneu und obwohl sie revolutionär ist – oder vielleicht gerade deswegen – wird das Ganze zunächst einige Überzeugungsarbeit erfordern. Ich habe in der **Fachpresse** damit für Aufmerksamkeit gesorgt und bekam dann einen Anruf von dieser Firma in Swansea, LSD Financial Services. Ich habe ihnen so viel Material über das System geschickt, wie ich hatte – darüber würde ich mit Ihnen gern reden, Steve. Es war nicht besonders gut. Haben wir denn nicht mehr? Vielleicht irgendetwas über den Erfolg des Systems in den Staaten?

S. Ich habe neues Material mitgebracht, aber hatte bisher noch keine Gelegenheit, es Ihnen zu geben. Es ist eine **hochaktuelle Broschüre**.

T. Großartig, das ist genau das, was ich brauche. Gut, dann lassen Sie mich Ihnen unsere **Strategie** für Swansea erklären …

Background Information

During the car journey to Swansea Trevor **fills** Steve and Peter **in** on the new software system, Quickpay. **To fill somebody in** means **to inform them, to give them all the news**.
Other »in« phrases include:

to tie in with	to be in agreement with
to let somebody in on	to allow somebody to be part of a secret
to go in for	to make a habit of doing something
to put in for	to apply for something (usually a job)
to stand in	to take the place of
to sleep in	to sleep later than usual
to come in for	to receive (usually criticism or blame)
to talk somebody into	to persuade
to take (it) out on	to make someone else suffer because of the way you feel

Train Yourself

Verwenden Sie nun diese »phrasal verbs« in den folgenden Sätzen!

1. Tony Dale ▬▬▬▬▬▬▬▬▬▬ for the sales director while the latter was at a sales conference.
2. Peter ▬▬▬▬▬▬▬▬▬▬ accompanying him to the trade fair even though I was laden down with work.
3. I hear you've ▬▬▬▬▬▬▬▬▬▬ Jeremy's old job. Do you think you'll get it?
4. My God! I know the boss is particularly stressed at the minute but I wish he wouldn't ▬▬▬▬▬▬▬▬▬▬ me!
5. I don't usually ▬▬▬▬▬▬▬▬▬▬ lunchtime drinking but this was an important client and so I ordered an expensive bottle of claret.

6. If I ▬▬▬▬▬ a secret, do you promise to tell nobody?
7. A meeting was held in order to ▬▬▬▬▬ everybody ▬▬▬▬▬ on the new changes that were about to take place.
8. I missed the connecting train to the airport because I ▬▬▬▬▬.
9. OK, all of this ▬▬▬▬▬ perfectly with the plans we made yesterday. I think we should go ahead.
10. The new proposals ▬▬▬▬▬ some harsh criticism from the press.

# Talk Talk Talk

T. We know LSD have been having problems with the security of their **account credit and debiting system**. They deal with so many banks and financial institutions and their business **is expanding** so rapidly that their present **mainframe** is overworked. This piece of software offers a gateway, a portal for all kinds of internet financial transactions while guaranteeing total security. Its **great selling point** is its one hundred per cent security. All credit information is held by the participating banks and finance houses. No **coding information**, no **enciphered data** gets onto the internet. This is what appeals to firms like LSD - you'll see what I mean when we meet their **CEO**.

T. Wir wissen, dass LSD Probleme mit der Sicherheit ihrer **Kreditkonten und Abbuchungssysteme** hat. Sie haben mit so vielen Banken und Finanzinstituten zu tun und ihr Geschäft **expandiert** so schnell, dass ihr derzeitiges **Computersystem** überlastet ist. Unsere Software bietet eine Art Durchgang, ein Portal zu allen möglichen finanziellen Transaktionen über das Internet an, während es absolute Sicherheit garantiert. Das **wichtigste Verkaufsargument** ist seine hundertprozentige Sicherheit. Alle Kreditinformationen bleiben bei den teilnehmenden Banken und Finanzhäusern. Es gibt keinerlei **kodierte Information**, keine **verschlüsselten Daten** gehen in das Internet hinaus. Genau das ist für Firmen wie LSD so ansprechend –

Sie werden verstehen, was ich meine, wenn wir ihren **CEO** treffen.

P. CEO?

P. CEO?

T. **Chief Executive Officer**. He's Welsh, like myself. David Powys is his name. You'll like him, he's OK. But he'll take some selling to ...

T. **Chief Executive Officer.** Er ist ein Waliser, genau wie ich. Sein Name ist David Powys. Sie werden ihn mögen, er ist in Ordnung. Aber auch er erfordert einige Überzeugungsarbeit ...

Background Information

Trevor says in this section of Talk Talk Talk that the **mainframe** at LSD is overworked. The **mainframe** is the central computer system. Other words and expressions with »**main**« include:

mainstay	the most important part of something providing support for everything else
domain	an area of interest over which a person has control
mainspring	the most important reason for something
mainstream	the way of life accepted by the most people
in the main	mostly
to maintain	to continue to keep/ have in existence

Train Yourself

Fügen Sie nun diese Wendungen in die Sätze ein!

1. The company's _____ was the microchip market, they were way ahead of their competitors.
2. _____ I get home from work at about ten at night although sometimes even later.

3. Tony was the ▒▒▒▒▒▒▒▒▒▒ of the operation, without him we would never have clinched the deal.
4. The ▒▒▒▒▒▒▒▒▒▒ to the company's success was the hard work put in by everybody.
5. When the ▒▒▒▒▒▒▒▒▒▒ crashed there was panic as it contained just about every important piece of information.
6. At present, the company ▒▒▒▒▒▒▒▒▒▒ five members of staff in the sales department and three in logistics.
7. To be successful in selling one must be aware of current ideas and fashions in ▒▒▒▒▒▒▒▒▒▒ culture.

 Talk Talk Talk

(The offices of LSD and Company, Trevor addresses the receptionist)

T. Good morning, we're here to see Mr Powys.

R. Is he expecting you?

T. Certainly. We have an **appointment** for 11 o'clock.

R. I'll call him ... Yes, Mr Powys is expecting you. If you'll follow me I'll take you to him now ...

(David Powys's office)

D. Good morning gentlemen! Did you have a good journey from Cardiff?

T. Fine, thank you Mr Powys. I'd like you to meet Steve Blackman, **Sales Director** of ERGO Limited,

(In den Büros von LSD, Trevor spricht eine Empfangsdame an)

T. Guten Morgen, wir möchten gern mit Mr Powys sprechen.

R. Erwartet er sie?

T. Natürlich. Wir haben einen Termin für 11 Uhr.

R. Ich werde ihn anrufen ... Ja, Mr Powys erwartet Sie. Wenn Sie mir bitte folgen, ich werde Sie gleich zu ihm führen ...

(David Powys Büro)

D. Guten Morgen, meine Herren! Hatten Sie eine gute Fahrt von Cardiff hierher?

T. Ja, danke, Mr Powys. Ich würde Ihnen gerne Steve Blackman, den **Verkaufsleiter** von ERGO Limited

and Mr Peter Brückner, the company's assistant managing Director.

und Mr Peter Brückner, den stellvertretenden Geschäftsführer der Firma vorstellen.

D. My, Trevor – I may call you Trevor? – you're **rolling out the heavy guns**. Is this such a hard sell?

D. Meine Güte, Trevor – ich darf Sie doch Trevor nennen? – Sie **fahren ja schwere Geschütze auf**. Rechnen Sie mit so harten Verkaufsgesprächen?

T. Steve and Peter are touring Britain, looking at our sales operation, and I thought it would be a good idea **to bring them along with me** today. Don't worry – **they're as new to Quickpay as you are** ...

T. Steve und Peter reisen durch England, um unsere Verkaufsstellen zu inspizieren und ich dachte, es wäre eine gute Idee, **sie heute mitzubringen**. Keine Sorge – **sie verstehen von Quickpay so wenig wie Sie** ...

Do's and Don'ts

British businessmen (such as David Powys) are often quick to move from a formal form of address to the informal use of first names. As **a rule of thumb**, wait for them to **enter** first **into first-name terms**. You'll usually be invited to communicate on that level – »Call me John! Let's drop this mister stuff!«

Background Information

Trevor says to David Powys that Steven and Peter are as **new to** Quickpay as he (David) is. The phrase »**new to**« is an example of a very common language structure in English – an adjective (new) plus a preposition (to). Other commonly used prepositional phrases comprising of an adjective with a preposition include:
interested in
worried about
good/bad at

wary of
concerned with/about
skilled in
disappointed in
impressed by
surprised by
pleased with
successful in

 Train Yourself

Verwenden Sie die oben stehenden Ausdrücke in den folgenden Sätzen:

1. We are very _____ the new marketing manager. She has settled into her new job very well.
2. The company were _____ the low profits shown by the new product. They were expecting a lot more consumer interest.
3. We are certainly very _____ your proposal and will be discussing it properly at the next board meeting.
4. He is _____ employing graduates without any experience at all of a working environment even if they are well-qualified.
5. We were very _____ your presentation this morning. It showed very thorough research into possible new markets for the new product.
6. He is _____ the technical side of his job but _____ any aspect involving communication skills.
7. The company has always been _____ predicting market trends. They have always foreseen the appearance of new directions.
8. She is very _____ negotiating with customers who are often difficult. She is always calm and diplomatic.
9. We are very _____ one of our colleagues who appears to have reacted very badly to the break-up of his marriage.
10. He's _____ the job so he still has a lot to learn.
11. We were _____ the results of the survey – we hadn't expected so much consumer interest.

12. We are ▧▧▧▧▧▧▧▧▧ the effect on the surrounding countryside of the new development and the possible reaction of local residents.

 **Talk Talk Talk**

(Still at the office)

T. Now, David, you've read all the brochure material we sent you, **I' take it** ...

D. If I hadn't, dear boy, you would not be sitting there now!

T. Then do you have any questions?

D. Certainly. I understand well enough how this software will organize our payments system. That just seems to be **an advance on** your **accounting program**, which – as you know – we have been **happily using** for some time now. In that respect, the Quickpay software is an update, a new generation of software ...

T. You are so right. You see, **you are getting double value** from this product ...

D. Good heavens, Steve – it is Steve isn't it? – this man of yours knows how to sell!

(Immer noch im Büro)

T. Also, David, **ich vermute,** Sie haben das Prospektmaterial, das wir Ihnen geschickt haben, gelesen ...

D. Wenn ich das nicht getan hätte, mein Lieber, würden Sie hier nicht sitzen!

T. Haben Sie irgendwelche Fragen?

D. Natürlich. Ich verstehe jetzt einigermaßen, wie diese Software unser Abbuchungssystem organisieren wird. Das scheint **eine Verbesserung** unseres Abrechnungsprogramms zu sein, das wir – wie Sie ja wissen – jetzt seit einiger Zeit **voller Zufriedenheit benutzen**. In dieser Hinsicht ist die Quickpay-Software ein Update, eine neue Generation von Software ...

T. Sie haben absolut Recht. Sehen Sie, **Sie profitieren** von diesem Produkt gleich **doppelt** ...

D. Du lieber Himmel, Steve – Ihr Name ist doch Steve, oder? – Ihr Kollege versteht es wirklich, etwas an den Mann zu bringen.

S. He's one of our best – but of course he is selling a **top product** here. No problem for him.

S. Er ist einer unserer besten Leute – aber natürlich verkauft er hier auch ein **Spitzenprodukt**. Das ist kein Problem für ihn.

Background Information

In this section of Talk Talk Talk David says his company have been **happily** using their accounting programme for some time. (The British use the American spelling of »programme« in context of computers.) »**Happily**« is an adverb corresponding to the adjective »**happy**«. As you know an adjective describes a noun whereas an adverb describes a verb. Below are other pairs of adverbs and adjectives:

warm – warmly	private – privately	direct – directly
accurate – accurately	anxious – anxiously	polite – politely
obvious – obviously	rapid – rapidly	unfailing – unfailingly

Train Yourself

Suchen Sie in den folgenden Sätzen das passende Wort in Klammern aus, um den Satz zu vervollständigen.

1. In business it is always better to deal ▓▓▓▓▓▓▓▓ *(direct/directly)* with the customer rather than going through a third party.
2. Although he publicly expressed interest in the merger, in ▓▓▓▓▓▓▓▓ *(private/privately)* he wasn't too sure.
3. On arriving at the conference we received a ▓▓▓▓▓▓▓▓ *(warm/warmly)* welcome from the organizers.
4. The company was ▓▓▓▓▓▓▓▓ *(unfailing/unfailingly)* in its attempts to float its shares on the stock market.
5. We waited ▓▓▓▓▓▓▓▓ *(anxious/anxiously)* for the results of the audit.
6. ▓▓▓▓▓▓▓▓ *(obvious/obviously)* it is better to do one's homework before meeting a client.

7. John said he would ▦▦▦▦▦ *(happy/happily)* do the job as long as he was paid expenses.
8. He rose ▦▦▦▦▦ *(rapid/rapidly)* through the ranks until he became CEO at the age of 40.
9. The company's forecast was not very ▦▦▦▦▦ *(accurate/accurately)* and as a result staff reductions were predicted.
10. In response to the customer complaint a ▦▦▦▦▦ *(polite/politely)* letter was sent offering a full apology.

 **Talk Talk Talk**

D. **What I'm not that clear about** is the security mechanism. We are very worried by this increasing number of internet fraud cases. We actually lost some **client details** only a few weeks ago – an **e-mailing retailer got hold of** them. Very embarrassing for us. I must admit **we are in the market now for** a really effective secure payments system. Now, tell me how yours works.

D. **Was ich noch nicht ganz verstehe**, ist diese Sicherheitseinrichtung. Wir sind sehr besorgt über diese zunehmenden Fälle von Internet-Verbrechen. Tatsache ist, dass wir erst vor ein paar Wochen einige **Kundendaten** verloren haben – **ein Händler von E-Mail-Adressen** hat sie **in die Finger bekommen**. Äußerst peinlich für uns. Ich muss zugeben, dass **wir jetzt wirklich Bedarf nach** einem effektiven Sicherheitssystem für Finanztransaktionen **haben**. Also, erzählen Sie mir, wie Ihres funktioniert.

T. First of all, we **move** all financial transaction handling **out of your control** and place it entirely in the hands of your bank. Your clients still believe they are dealing with you but in effect they and you are enjoying the complete security of the bank. One major High Street bank, by the way, is already using our system, but all banks now

T. Zunächst einmal **nehmen** wir alle finanziellen Transaktionen **aus ihrem Verantwortungsbereich heraus** und legen sie voll und ganz in die Hände Ihrer Bank. Ihre Kunden werden immer noch glauben, es mit Ihnen zu tun zu haben, obwohl sie in Wirklichkeit in den Genuss der vollen Sicherheit der Bank kommen. Eine der großen Banken

have pretty **foolproof security shields**.

D. So tell me more about yours – why it's better than the rest.

T. Well, let me tell you how it functions and you'll soon see why we are **leaders** in this field …

in der High Street benutzt übrigens schon unser System, aber mittlerweile haben alle Banken ziemlich **narrensichere Sicherheitssperren**.

D. Dann erzählen Sie mir mehr über Ihres – warum es besser als die anderen ist.

T. Na schön, lassen Sie mich erklären, wie es funktioniert und Sie werden schon bald verstehen, warum wir die **Marktführer** in diesem Bereich sind …

Background Information

David Powys in this section of the dialogue tells Steve and Peter about how an **e-mailing retailer got hold of** some client details causing him to be concerned about the company's security mechanism. In this context »**to get hold of**« means **to find something and use it**; it can also mean **to contact somebody**, e.g. »Did you get hold of Jeremy yesterday?« or **to take something in one's hands** »He got hold of the rope and pulled«. In this instance it is the first meaning we are concerned with.

Phrasal verbs and expressions with »**hold**« include:

to hold up	to delay
to hold with	to agree (usually with an idea)
to hold out	to offer (usually hope)
to hold forth	to speak for a long time (often pompously)
to hold one's own	to continue to defend oneself in a difficult situation
to hold one's breath	to wait anxiously for something
to get hold of the wrong end of the stick	to misunderstand something completely

| to hold the fort | to look after a business or state of affairs while someone is away |

 Train Yourself

Ergänzen Sie folgende Sätze und verwenden Sie dazu obige Wendungen:

1. Have you heard about Michael leaving the company at the end of the year? Don't ▓▓▓▓▓▓▓▓▓▓. He's only thinking about it.
2. The managing director left his assistant to ▓▓▓▓▓▓▓▓▓▓ while he was away.
3. Sorry I'm late. I was ▓▓▓▓▓▓▓▓▓▓ in traffic.
4. I don't really ▓▓▓▓▓▓▓▓▓▓ the idea that staff should be asked to retire at 60.
5. At the conference the organizer ▓▓▓▓▓▓▓▓▓▓ for 45 minutes causing some delegates to nearly fall asleep!
6. Management don't ▓▓▓▓▓▓▓▓▓▓ much hope that the dispute will be settled by the end of the week.
7. You seem to have ▓▓▓▓▓▓▓▓▓▓! I never said I would be leaving the company! I said I was leaving to go on holiday!
8. My P.A. tried for half an hour to ▓▓▓▓▓▓▓▓▓▓ him but was constantly told to just hold the line.
9. The company seems to be ▓▓▓▓▓▓▓▓▓▓ despite the economic climate.
10. Somebody ▓▓▓▓▓▓▓▓▓▓ some sensitive information and is causing enormous headaches for the management.

 Talk Talk Talk

(The hotel bar) | (In der Hotelbar)

S. I'm impressed, Trevor. You witnessed a good salesman at work today, Peter.

S. Ich bin beeindruckt, Trevor. Sie haben heute einen guten Verkäufer bei der Arbeit gesehen, Peter.

P. I know. I was also very impressed. It was very interesting, after all this theory, to see **sales techniques** put into practice.

T. Thanks, gents – but you gave me great support. I think Powys was also impressed – but by the heavyweight team we rolled out.

S. Like one of your famous rugby sides, eh, Trevor!

T. Actually, Steve, rugby and selling have some things in common. Believe me, I used to play for a crack Swansea side. Strategy is **of paramount importance**, for a start. You don't take the field without being fully prepared, with an action plan in your head. **Tactics are secondary.** Look at a **sales pitch** as another rugby ground. Know your strengths but also your weaknesses – there's nearly always a weak link. You have to find it and compensate for it. Then you have to know your opposition just about as well as you know yourself. Respect your opposition, too. Don't just **rubbish** the other side or its products. If you're selling, admit that there are similar, good products out there in the market place. Prove that your product is better.

P. Ich weiß. Ich war auch sehr beeindruckt. Nach der ganzen Theorie war es sehr interessant, die **Verkaufstechniken** einmal in die Praxis umgesetzt zu sehen.

T. Danke, Herrschaften – aber Sie haben mich auch großartig unterstützt. Ich glaube, auch Powys war beeindruckt – von dem hochkarätigen Team, mit dem wir angerollt sind.

S. Wie eines Ihrer berühmten Rugby-Teams, was, Trevor?!

T. Streng genommen, Steve, haben Rugby und der Verkauf einiges gemeinsam. Glauben Sie mir das, ich habe für ein erstklassiges Team aus Swansea gespielt. Zunächst einmal ist die Strategie **von entscheidender Bedeutung**. Man geht nicht aufs Spielfeld, ohne lückenlos vorbereitet zu sein, mit einem genauen Handlungsplan im Kopf. Die **Taktik ist dann zweitrangig**. Betrachten Sie ein **Verkaufsgespräch** als ein Rugby-Spielfeld. Kennen Sie Ihre Stärken, aber auch Ihre Schwächen – und es gibt fast immer eine Schwachstelle. Sie müssen sie erkennen und einen Ausgleich dafür suchen. Und dann müssen Sie auch Ihren Gegner so gut kennen wie sich selbst. Sie sollten Ihren Gegner auch respektieren. **Werten** Sie die Gegenseite oder ihre Produkte nicht einfach nur **ab**.

P. I noticed you **adopted that approach** when you told David Powys banks are using systems that we did not supply.

P. Mir ist aufgefallen, dass Sie **diesen Ansatz benutzt** haben, als Sie David Powys sagten, dass Banken auch Systeme benutzen, die nicht von uns geliefert werden.

T. No sense in hiding that fact. He would discover it anyway, and then our **credibility** would be damaged or even destroyed. **Honesty pays in selling**, believe me!

T. Es hätte keinen Sinn gemacht, diese Tatsache zu verschweigen. Er hätte es so oder so herausgefunden und unsere **Glaubwürdigkeit** wäre damit angeschlagen oder sogar zerstört worden. **Ehrlichkeit im Verkauf zahlt sich aus**, glauben Sie mir!

Wenn Sie etwas verkaufen, müssen Sie auch eingestehen, dass es ähnliche gute Produkte auf dem Markt gibt. Beweisen Sie, dass Ihr Produkt besser ist.

S. We believe you, and I'm sure Powys did, too. Now what are we drinking?

S. Wir glauben Ihnen und ich bin sicher, dass Powys das auch getan hat. Also, was wollen wir trinken?

 Background Information

»**Honesty pays in selling**« according to Trevor, meaning that **it is advantageous to do so**. He could have said »**honesty pays dividends**«, another expression with the same meaning.
Let's look at some more »**pay**« expressions:

to pay lip-service	to say that one approves of or supports something while not doing anything about it
to pay the price for	to suffer because of a previous error or wrongdoing

to pay through the nose	to pay a very high price for something
to pay attention to	to take careful notice of
to pay off	when a risky course of action proves successful
to put paid to something	to stop or destroy something
there'll be hell to pay	informal expression meaning great trouble will result

 **Train Yourself**

Verwenden Sie obige Wendungen in folgenden Sätzen:

1. The company ▓▓▓▓▓▓▓▓▓▓ for a lack of investment when share prices plummeted (fell heavily).
2. ▓▓▓▓▓▓▓▓▓▓ if we lose this account!
3. Knowing one's strengths and weaknesses ▓▓▓▓▓▓▓▓▓▓ when one meets the client.
4. The company ▓▓▓▓▓▓▓▓▓▓ for their new security systems - the cost was far higher than expected.
5. The management ▓▓▓▓▓▓▓▓▓▓ to the idea without being convinced about its benefits.
6. The gamble ▓▓▓▓▓▓▓▓▓▓ when the deal was finally clinched and there was champagne all round to celebrate.
7. The economic crisis ▓▓▓▓▓▓▓▓▓▓ any plans the company had for expansion.
8. If a salesperson wants to learn the ropes he or she must ▓▓▓▓▓▓▓▓▓▓ to the advice of more experienced colleagues.

 Talk Talk Talk

(The next day. The hotel's breakfast room)	(Am nächsten Tag. Im Frühstücksraum des Hotels)
S. Good morning, Peter. How are you feeling today?	S. Guten Morgen, Peter. Wie geht es Ihnen heute?

P. I shouldn't have had that third pint, Steve. I've got **a bit of a hangover**.	P. Ich hätte das dritte Pint nicht trinken sollen, Steve. Ich habe **einen kleinen Kater**.
S. You know my hangover cure? **Kippers**. They're over there on the buffet table.	S. Kennen Sie mein Heilmittel gegen Kater? **Kippers**. Da drüben am Buffet gibt es welche.
P. Kippers?	P. Kippers?
S. Smoked fish, dear boy! You must have eaten them in Hamburg.	S. Geräucherter Fisch (Bückling), mein Lieber. So etwas müssen Sie in Hamburg doch auch gegessen haben.
P. The only fish I ate in Hamburg were fresh, apart from pickled herring - Matjes. Have you ever tried those?	P. In Hamburg habe ich immer nur frischen Fisch gegessen, mal abgesehen von eingelegten Heringen – Matjes. Haben Sie die mal probiert?
S. Sounds dreadful. No, **I'll stick to kippers** - you should try them, too ...	S. Klingt furchtbar! Nein, **ich bleibe bei den Kippers** – Sie sollten sie auch einmal probieren ...
(A hotel employee approaches the table)	(Ein Hotelangestellter tritt an den Tisch)
E. Excuse me, sir. Are you Mr Blackman?	E. Entschuldigen Sie, Sir. Sind Sie Mr Blackman?
S. That's me.	S. Das bin ich.
E. I have a Mr Jones on the phone. He says it's urgent.	E. Ich habe einen Mr Jones am Apparat. Er sagt, es wäre dringend.
S. I'll be right there. Excuse me, Peter ...	S. Ich komme sofort. Entschuldigen Sie mich, Peter ...

Do's and Don'ts

A reminder for **business travellers** in Britain: when booking a hotel always make sure it serves a full English breakfast, a buffet if possible. And check whether it is included in the room rate. A full English breakfast will **keep** the busy businessman **going** all day - there's no need even to break for the proverbial business lunch! And if kippers are on the breakfast menu **give them a try**!

Background Information

Steve doesn't like the sound of Matjes, he says he'd rather **stick to** kippers. To »**stick to**« means to stay with something. Other phrases and expressions with »**stick**« include:

to stick one's neck out	to take a risk
to get hold of the wrong end of the stick	to misunderstand something
a stick-in-the-mud	a person who has fixed ideas and is unadventurous
to carry a big stick (over)	to use power or to enforce control strictly
to stick in one's oar	to try to concern oneself in the affairs of others
to stick to one's guns	to continue to support a particular course of action
to stick out like a sore thumb	to be totally out of place

Train Yourself

Setzen Sie die Wendungen in die folgenden Sätze ein!

1. The management decided to ▬▬▬▬▬▬▬▬ and go ahead with the takeover despite widespread protest.
2. I hadn't realized the dinner was going to be so formal and I ▬▬▬▬▬▬▬▬.

3. It's impossible to come to any decisions at a meeting when everybody tries to ▓▓▓▓▓▓▓▓▓▓▓▓▓▓▓▓▓▓▓▓▓▓.
4. The company didn't want to be thought of as ▓▓ and so decided to take a risk.
5. I listened intently to the agenda for next week's meetings just so that I didn't ▓▓▓▓▓▓▓▓▓▓▓▓▓▓▓▓▓▓▓▓▓▓
6. I don't think we're off-course here, I think we should ▓▓▓▓▓▓▓▓▓▓▓▓▓▓▓▓▓▓▓▓▓▓▓▓▓▓▓▓ our present plan of action.
7. The new sales manager ▓▓▓▓▓▓▓▓▓▓▓▓▓▓▓▓▓▓▓▓▓▓▓▓▓▓ and issued a series of company policy statements to all members of staff.
8. I think we should ▓▓▓▓▓▓▓▓▓▓▓▓▓▓▓▓▓▓▓▓▓▓▓▓▓▓ on this one. If we don't take a risk, we'll regret it later.

Talk Talk Talk

(Steve returns to the table)

S. You're not going to believe this, Peter!

P. What did Trevor Jones have to tell you?

S. Do you want the good news first or the bad news?

P. This early in the day **I'll go for** the bad news.

S. Trevor told me David Powys called him first thing this morning and said a **hacker** had **broken into** their system and stolen credit card information on more than 1,000 clients. There's mayhem today over at LSD. Poor old Trevor was practically weeping. He's **in a heck of a state**!

(Steve kehrt an den Tisch zurück)

S. Sie werden das nicht glauben, Peter!

P. Was wollte Trevor Jones denn?

S. Wollen Sie zuerst die gute oder die schlechte Nachricht hören?

P. So früh am Morgen **ziehe ich** die schlechte Nachricht **vor**.

S. Trevor hat mir erzählt, dass David Powys gleich heute Morgen angerufen hat und sagte, dass ein **Hacker** in ihr System **eingebrochen** wäre und Kreditkarteninformationen von mehr als 1000 Kunden gestohlen hat. Drüben bei LSD herrscht das absolute Chaos. Der arme alte Trevor war fast am

P. Good Lord! That's terrible. The nightmare of every company. So what's the good news?

S. Powys wants our system installed right away. He didn't even ask for a **cost estimate**. Trevor is down there right now - it's the biggest **sale** he's made yet.

P. And what do we do?

S. We're off to Scotland, boyo! With that contract **under our belts** we've got a great head start. How were the kippers?

Heulen. Er ist **in einem furchtbaren Zustand**!

P. Mein Gott! Das ist ja entsetzlich. Der Alptraum jeder Firma. Und was sind die guten Nachrichten?

S. Powys will unser System sofort installiert haben. Er hat nicht einmal nach einem **Kostenvoranschlag** gefragt. Trevor ist schon rübergefahren - das ist sein bisher größter **Geschäftsabschluss**.

P. Und was machen wir?

S. Wir brechen auf nach Schottland, Kumpel! Mit diesem Vertrag **unter Dach und Fach** haben wir einen großartigen Start hingelegt. Wie waren die Bücklinge?

Background Information

A hacker has broken into the computer system of the company visited by Steve and Peter. If a hacker breaks into a computer system he or she penetrates its security system and gains access to files. »Break« is a verb with many additional meanings – many of them in the world of business and industry.

Train Yourself

Versuchen Sie nun »break« in den folgenden Sätzen korrekt zu verwenden. Benutzen Sie hierfür die folgenden Optionen: *broke the back, break the market, break the strike, break even, make or break, break.*

1. The company disregarded the terms of the contract and ▓▓▓▓▓▓ ▓▓▓▓▓▓▓▓▓▓▓ the agreement.

2. The costs were crippling for the company. They finally ▮▮▮▮ the management's ▮▮▮▮.
3. For a few years after its foundation, the company had an upward struggle. It was ▮▮▮▮.
4. The share price dropped so low that it threatened to ▮▮▮▮
5. The company managed to balance income and outgoings. It ▮▮▮▮ ▮▮▮▮.
6. The unions were not strong enough to continue the work stoppage. Management managed to ▮▮▮▮

 Vocabulary

account credit	Kreditkonten
accounting program	Abrechnungsprogramm
to adopt an approach	einen Ansatz benutzen
advance	Fortschritt
a lot of scope	ein breites Betätigungsfeld
appointment	Termin, Verabredung
to be in the market for	wirklich Bedarf haben nach
client details	Kundendaten
cost estimate	Kostenvoranschlag
easy-going	unkompliziert
enciphered data	verschlüsselte Daten
to expand	expandieren
to fill sb. in	jdn. ins Bild setzen
financial exchange software	Bilanzierungsprogramm
financial services company	Finanzdienstleister
to fire away	losschießen (ugs.)
to get double value from sth.	von etw. doppelt profitieren
to get hold of sth.	etw. in die Finger bekommen
to go for sth.	etw. vorziehen
Honesty pays in selling!	Ehrlichkeit zahlt sich im Verkauf aus!
in a heck of a state	in einem furchtbaren Zustand
It will take some selling.	Es wird einige harte Verkaufsgespräche geben.
kipper	Bückling

leader	hier: Marktführer
mainframe	Computersystem
of paramount importance	von entscheidender Bedeutung
one-man operation	Ein-Mann-Betrieb
out and about	unterwegs
to pay dividends	sich bezahlt machen
to roll out the heavy guns	schwere Geschütze auffahren
to rubbish	abwerten
sale	Geschäftsabschluss
sales area	Verkaufsbereich
salespeople	Außendienstmitarbeiter
secondary	zweitrangig
selling point	Verkaufsargument
(to) show sb. the ropes	jdm. etw. erklären (ugs.)
to stick to	hier: bleiben bei
trade press	Fachpresse
under our belts	unter Dach und Fach
up-to-date	hochaktuell

Place proposals
Angebote unterbreiten

 Here we go

Peter und Steve befinden sich immer noch auf ihrer Rundreise durch die verschiedenen Verkaufsvertretungen von ERGO Limited. Sie sind gerade in Schottland angekommen, um sich mit Angus Fairbairn, ERGOs Mann, in Glasgow zu treffen. Zusammen mit ihm wird Peter Einblicke in das neue »Online-Geschäft« und in so genannte »Cyber Parks«, neue Online-Geschäftszentren, erhalten. Außerdem findet Peter gefallen an Schottland, dem dortigen Lebensstil und den freundlichen Menschen. Es gibt noch viel Neues kennen zu lernen ...

 **Talk Talk Talk**

(The hotel lobby)

S. All **ready for off**, Peter?

P. Just **say the word**, Steve.

S. The car's waiting. I've paid the bill, called the office, told James the good news. Now let's conquer Scotland. Let's go ...

(In the car)

S. We'll **break the journey** in the Lake District. Glasgow is our first destination. We have two offices in

(Die Hotel-Lobby)

S. Sind Sie **fertig zum Aufbruch**, Peter?

P. **Wann immer Sie wollen**, Steve.

S. Der Wagen wartet. Ich habe die Rechnung bezahlt, im Büro angerufen und James die gute Nachricht überbracht. Lassen Sie uns Schottland erobern. Los geht's ...

(Im Wagen)

S. Im nordwestlichen Seengebiet **unterbrechen** wir **unsere Reise**. Unser erstes Ziel ist Glasgow.

Scotland, you know – one in Glasgow and the other in Edinburgh. Business has picked up since **devolution**. The Scots seem to be flourishing under independence – well, semi-independence.

Wissen Sie, wir haben zwei Büros in Schottland – eines in Glasgow und das andere in Edinburgh. Die Geschäfte dort haben seit der **Dezentralisierung** angezogen. Die Schotten scheinen aufzublühen in ihrer Unabhängigkeit – na ja, Halbunabhängigkeit.

Background Information

1. Scotland and Wales were granted a form of independence in 1999. Scotland now has a Parliament with sweeping powers, while Wales has a National Assembly with a more limited form of independence. The process of granting the two regions semi-independence is described as **devolution**.

2. Steve wants **to break the journey** to Scotland by stopping in the Lake District. In this context **breaking the journey** means **to interrupt** it. There are various phrases and expressions with **break** in English, some of them are listed below:

to break off	to stop talking
to break down	to stop working
to break up	to come to an end
a breakthrough	an important discovery that helps to provide an answer to a problem
to break in (coll.)	to prepare or train
to break even	to have one's losses balanced by one's gains
to break new ground	to do something new or to make a discovery
to break the back of something	to complete the most difficult part of a job
to break the ice	to make a formal or nervous situation easier by a friendly act or conversation

 **Train Yourself**

Setzen Sie die »phrasal verbs« nun in die folgenden Sätze ein!

1. The company is ▬▬▬▬▬▬▬ by opening a new branch in the Czech Republic.
2. I've got a really heavy workload on at the moment. Why don't we meet tonight at my place and try to ▬▬▬▬▬▬▬ it?
3. Everybody felt nervous at the party until Tony ▬▬▬▬▬▬▬ by telling one of his famous bad jokes.
4. There was a minor crisis at work when the photocopier ▬▬▬▬▬▬▬ .
5. The best management can hope for is that the company will ▬▬▬▬▬▬▬ at the end of the year.
6. The meeting finally ▬▬▬▬▬▬▬ at midnight.
7. I'm ▬▬▬▬▬▬▬ my new P.A. at the moment, just showing her the ropes, you know.
8. After days of negotiations the two sides in the dispute finally came to a ▬▬▬▬▬▬▬ and the problem was solved.
9. During the interview the Sales Director ▬▬▬▬▬▬▬ to attend to an important phone call.
10. I'm exhausted! Let's ▬▬▬▬▬▬▬ the journey and get some lunch!

Talk Talk Talk

(Dining room of motel on road between Carlisle and Glasgow)

S. Sorry about the Lake District, Peter. I didn't expect all hotels to be full. We should have called **beforehand** to book. It is a weekend, of course.

(Speisezimmer im Motel an der Straße zwischen Carlisle und Glasgow)

S. Peter, das mit dem Seengebiet tut mir leid. Ich hatte nicht erwartet, dass alle Hotels voll belegt sein würden. Wir hätten **vorher** anrufen und buchen sollen. Es ist schließlich Wochenende.

P. Not to worry, Steve. We shall be comfortable enough here, and we'll have time enough for sightseeing when this trip is over. Tell me now what awaits us tomorrow.	P. Ärgern Sie sich nicht, Steve. Wir haben es hier bequem genug und noch genügend Zeit für die Sehenswürdigkeiten, wenn diese Reise vorbei ist. Erzählen Sie mir jetzt, was uns morgen erwartet.
S. Glasgow is **making a big bid** to become one of Europe's new »**cyber cities**«. A centre for high-tech business and industry. Its old industrial and shipbuilding base has all but vanished. Glasgow was one of the first centres of the **industrial revolution**. It doesn't want to be left behind by the **new revolution**.	S. Glasgow **bemüht sich sehr**, Europas neue »**Cyber-City**« zu werden. Ein Zentrum für Hightech-Geschäfte und Industrie. Die frühere Handelsbasis Industrie- und Schiffbau ist völlig verschwunden. Glasgow war eines der ersten Zentren der **industriellen Revolution**. Es möchte von der **neuen Revolution** nicht zurückgelassen werden.
P. So where do we come in?	P. Und wo kommen wir ins Spiel?
S. Our job is to help local business and industry achieve their ambition to be leaders in this new revolution. We have the products. We just have to persuade Glasgow companies that **it's worth their while** buying them.	S. Unsere Aufgabe ist es, dem örtlichen Handel und der Industrie dabei zu helfen, dass sie ihre Ziele erreichen und die Anführer dieser neuen Revolution werden. Wir haben die Produkte. Wir müssen lediglich die Glasgower Unternehmen davon überzeugen, dass **sie es wert sind**, gekauft zu werden.
P. And how do we do that?	P. Und wie machen wir das?
S. You'll see tomorrow when you meet Angus Fairbairn, our Glasgow **representative**.	S. Das werden Sie morgen schon sehen, wenn wir uns mit Angus Fairbairn, unserem Glasgower **Repräsentanten**, treffen.

Background Information

Steve apologizes to Peter for not being able to find accommodation in the Lake District.
He says he should have called **beforehand** to reserve rooms.
»Beforehand« means **before something else has happened**, in this case before they arrived in the Lake District.
There are many other phrases and expressions with »**hand**«, let's look at some of them:

to have the upper hand	to have a position of power or control over someone
to put one's hand to	to begin or try to do a task or job
out of hand	out of control
to know something/somewhere like the back of one's hand	to know it very well
to show one's hand	to do or say something that reveals one's intentions
an old hand	a person with a long experience in a job or activity
to go hand in hand	to be connected or closely related
at first hand	directly with the person or operation involved
underhand	dishonest and usually done secretly

Train Yourself

Verwenden Sie diese Wendungen nun in den folgenden Sätzen!

1. Steve and Peter are touring around the offices of ERGO Ltd to see things ▬▬▬▬▬▬▬▬▬▬▬▬▬ .
2. Joseph is ▬▬▬▬▬▬▬▬▬▬▬▬▬ at the job. He's been here twenty years.
3. When negotiating deals it's vitally important not to ▬▬▬▬▬▬▬▬▬▬▬▬▬▬▬▬▬▬ too early.

4. The stationery budget is getting ▓▓▓▓▓▓▓▓▓▓▓▓▓▓▓▓▓▓▓▓▓ !
   Could people please not waste paper.
5. Steve volunteered to show Peter and Trevor around the town as he
   ▓▓▓▓▓▓▓▓▓▓▓▓▓▓▓▓▓▓ .
6. You should have rung me ▓▓▓▓▓▓▓▓▓▓▓▓▓▓▓▓▓▓▓▓ . I can't
   really see you at the moment.
7. George is so flexible, he is always ready to ▓▓▓▓▓▓▓▓▓▓▓▓
   ▓▓▓▓▓▓▓▓▓▓▓▓▓▓▓▓▓▓▓▓ anything that comes his way.
8. Good salesmanship ▓▓▓▓▓▓▓▓▓▓▓▓▓▓▓▓▓▓▓ with confidence
   and belief in the product.
9. The management were accused by the union of being ▓▓▓▓▓▓▓▓
    ▓▓▓▓▓▓▓▓▓▓▓▓▓▓▓▓▓ in their dealings with workers.
10. To ▓▓▓▓▓▓▓▓▓▓▓▓▓▓▓▓▓▓▓ in the market we need to be
    cost-effective, otherwise we will lose clients.

Talk Talk Talk

(In the car, entering Glasgow)

(Im Auto, beim Eintreffen in Glasgow)

S. We'll **make straight for** the office. Angus is waiting there for us ... Here we are. Our office is on the third floor. **Mind how you go.** They're renovating the lobby. Glasgow is one huge building site at the moment. It was recently Europe's »City of Architecture« – and the building seems to be still going on!
(Enters office) Angus, dear boy!

How are you? How good to see you again. **How's business**?

A. Mustn't grumble. But I'm making no promises, you know.

S. Wir machen uns **sofort auf zum** Büro. Angus wartet dort auf uns ... Hier ist es. Unser Büro ist im dritten Stock. **Passen Sie auf, wo Sie hintreten.** Die Lobby wird gerade renoviert. Glasgow ist momentan eine einzige große Baugrube. Vor kurzem war es Europas »Stadt der Architektur« und die Bautätigkeit scheint immer noch weiterzugehen!
(Betritt das Büro) Angus, mein Bester!
Guten Tag! Schön, Sie wieder zu sehen. **Wie gehen die Geschäfte**?

A. Kann nicht klagen. Aber versprechen kann ich nichts, wissen Sie.

S. **Canny** Scot, this Angus – be warned, Peter. Oh, Angus! This is Peter Brückner, our Assistant Managing Director, over from Germany.	S. Ein **vorsichtiger** Schotte, dieser Angus – seien Sie gewarnt, Peter. Oh, Angus! Das ist Peter Brückner, unser stellvertretender Geschäftsführer aus Deutschland.
A. Germany? Welcome to Scotland, Peter. Been here before?	A. Deutschland? Willkommen in Schottland, Peter. Schon mal hier gewesen?
P. No my first visit. But I hope to be able to acquaint myself well with the country during this visit.	P. Nein, das ist mein erster Besuch. Aber ich hoffe, ich werde es schaffen, während meines Aufenthalts etwas von dem Land kennen zu lernen.
A. You'll see something of the Lowlands tomorrow, but the Highlands will have to wait. You'll have to come back.	A. Morgen werden Sie einen Teil des Tieflandes sehen, aber das Hochland wird noch warten müssen. Sie müssen unbedingt wieder kommen.
S. What's the Lowlands trip?	S. Worum geht es bei dem Trip ins Tiefland?
A. There are plans for a so-called **cyber-park** there. Big **subsidies** and **tax breaks** are being offered to new **IT companies setting up**. Our job is to make sure they are aware of the software and servicing support we can **provide**.	A. Es gibt Pläne bezüglich eines so genannten »Cyber-Park«s. Neuen **IT-Gesellschaften** werden hohe **Subventionen** und **Steuerunterbrechungen** angeboten, damit sie **sich** dort **niederlassen**. Unsere Aufgabe ist es, dafür zu sorgen, dass sie die Software- und Serviceleistungen kennen, die wir **bereitstellen** können.
S. That's a big undertaking.	S. Das ist eine gewaltige Aufgabe.

A. We go right to the heart of the operation. I have an appointment tomorrow with the planning and management board. You'll be there, too, of course.

S. As long as we're not in the way.

A. Not as long as Peter is there. A German as part of the team can't do any harm!

A. Wir setzen direkt im Herzen des Vorhabens an. Morgen habe ich eine Verabredung mit dem Planungs- und Leitungsausschuss. Sie werden natürlich dabei sein.

S. So lange wir dabei nicht im Weg stehen.

A. Nicht so lange Peter dabei ist. Ein Deutscher als Teil des Teams kann nicht schaden!

Background Information

In »cyberspeak«, **IT** stands for **Information Technology**. Here are some others from the **IT-vocabulary**:

ISP	Internet Service Provider
MSE	Medium and Small-sized Enterprises. Most of the new IT companies fall into this category
R&D	Research and Development. An R&D budget is an amount of money set aside by a company for the purpose of research and development of a product.
e-Commerce	electronic commerce, or the »business« of doing business electronically

E-Commerce is based on the **electronic processing and transmission of data**, including text, sound and video. It encompasses many diverse elements, including the electronic trading of goods and services, the online delivery of digital material, transfer of funds, share trading, auctions, direct consumer marketing and after-sales servicing - literally everything covered by the general term »business«!

Background Information

Steve says to Peter, »**Mind how you go**« when they arrive at the office building.

»To **mind** something« is to pay attention to it. Other phrases with »mind« include:

to bear in mind	to remember or continue to consider
to be in two minds	to be undoubtful or uncertain about sth.
to make up one's mind	to decide
to have something in mind	to intend to do sth.
to know one's mind	to know what one wants, to have clear and firm opinions
to speak one's mind	to speak honestly and openly
to slip one's mind	to forget something
to cross one's mind	to happen to come into one's thoughts
to set one's mind to something	to put all one's efforts into doing something

Train Yourself

Fünf der folgenden Sätze haben Fehler. **Finden und berichtigen Sie sie!**

1. Before we get too optimistic about competing in the Japanese market one must bear in mind that this is virgin territory for us.

2. After months of deliberations management have finally crossed their minds to go ahead with the project.

3. – Peter, I'd like you to do an important job for us.
   – Yes, Mr Morgan, what exactly did you make up your mind?

4. Jenny is known for slipping her mind. If she's not careful she'll land herself in trouble one of these days.

5. – The thought crossed my mind that we need to diversify a little more.

6. He made up his mind to improve his computer skills and decided to enroll on a course immediately.

7. – Oh Peter, it nearly spoke my mind. I need those reports by Friday.

8. The company was knowing their minds about going ahead with the proposal or not.

Colloquial English

> A **canny** person is somebody who thinks quickly and cleverly, especially in business or financial matters.

 Talk Talk Talk

(At the »Cyber-park« central offices)

(In den »Cyber-Park«-Hauptbüros)

A. OK, lads, **let me do the talking**. If there's anything you want to contribute wait until we have a break and then let's discuss it.

A. Okay, **lassen Sie mich das Reden übernehmen**. Falls Sie irgendetwas beitragen wollen, warten Sie, bis wir eine Pause machen und lassen Sie es uns diskutieren.

S. What did I tell you, Peter? A canny Scot!

S. Was habe ich Ihnen gesagt, Peter? Ein vorsichtiger Schotte!

A. Now come on, Steve. I've learnt a lot from you. Right, let's go in.

A. Jetzt kommen Sie schon, Steve. Ich habe viel von Ihnen gelernt! In

	Ordnung, lassen Sie uns reingehen.
(The three enter the offices. Receptionist greets them)	(Die drei betreten die Büros. Der Mann am Empfang begrüßt sie)
R. Good morning, gentlemen! Can I be of assistance?	R. Guten Morgen, meine Herren! Kann ich Ihnen behilflich sein?
A. We have an **appointment** with the Managing Director, Mr Travis.	A. Wir haben einen **Termin** mit dem leitenden Direktor, Mr. Travis.
R. Of course, you must be Mr Fairbairn, from ERGO …	R. Natürlich, Sie müssen Mr. Fairbairn von ERGO sein …
A. And these are my colleagues, Mr Blackman, our **Sales Chief**, and Mr Brückner, our Assistant Managing director.	A. Und das sind meine Kollegen, Mr. Blackman, unser **Verkaufsleiter** und Mr. Brückner, unser stellvertretender Geschäftsführer.
R. Please follow me. Mr Travis is waiting in his office.	R. Bitte folgen Sie mir. Mr. Travis wartet in seinem Büro.
(The three enter Travis's office)	(Die drei betreten Mr. Travis Büro)
T. Good morning, gentlemen. You found us without difficulty?	T. Guten Morgen, meine Herren. Haben Sie gut zu uns gefunden?
A. Yes, thank you. May I introduce Mr Blackman and Mr Brückner, both from London.	A. Ja, danke. Darf ich Ihnen Mr. Blackman und Mr. Brückner aus London vorstellen.
T. Pleased to meet you. Now **down to business**. How does ERGO propose to help us **get** this operation **off the ground**?	T. Freut mich, Sie kennen zu lernen. **Kommen wir zum Geschäftlichen**. Welche Art von Hilfestellung kann uns ERGO bieten, um das Geschäft **in Gang zu bringen**?

Background Information

Mr Travis asks Angus how he can help his company **get** the operation **off the ground**, i.e. **to get something started** or **to put something into operation**. Let's look at some other expressions with »**ground**«.

to have grounds for (doing something)	to have a reason, justification
to cut the ground from under someone's feet	to spoil someone's argument or plan by anticipating it
to break new ground	to introduce or discover a new method or system
common ground	opinions or experiences shared by two or more people
to cover a lot of ground	to deal with many different subjects very thoroughly
to fall on stony ground	not to be listened to or taken notice of
to gain ground	to advance or make progress
to have one's feet firmly on the ground	to be realistic or practical
a happy hunting ground	a place where a person finds what he desires or is very successful

Train Yourself

Benutzen Sie die oben stehenden Wendungen in den folgenden Sätzen!

1. The north-east is a very ▨▨▨▨▨▨▨▨▨▨▨ for us. We always sell well up there.
2. It took three months to finally get the project ▨▨▨▨▨▨▨▨▨▨▨ due to frequent delays.
3. Our competitor ▨▨▨▨▨▨▨▨▨▨▨ when they introduced an almost identical system to ours.

4. The new computer security system will ▓▓▓▓▓ when it is launched. In the UK it is the first of its kind.
5. Tony's proposition for more parking spaces to be made available to junior staff ▓▓▓▓▓. The chairman swiftly moved on to the next matter on the agenda.
6. You can rely on Debbie to get things done with the minimum of fuss. She ▓▓▓▓▓.
7. If we want to ▓▓▓▓▓ on our competitors we're all going to have to make a supreme effort this year.
8. Establishing ▓▓▓▓▓ with a client is a good foundation for a successful sale.
9. The boss ▓▓▓▓▓ no ▓▓▓▓▓ for taking it out on us! We did the best we possibly could!
10. The meeting was very constructive and we ▓▓▓▓▓.

 Talk Talk Talk

(Still at »Cyber Park«)

(Immer noch im »Cyber Park«)

A. Now, as I understand it, you'll have **broadband communications** here. Fibre optics?

A. Nun, so weit ich Sie verstehe, werden Sie hier über **Breitband-Kommunikation** verfügen. Fieberglas?

T. Yes, the **preparatory work** has begun.

T. Ja, die **Vorbereitungen** haben bereits begonnen.

A. What ERGO is proposing is that we **come in on the ground-floor**, assisting you at every stage. We have **a broad palette** of programs, each suited to **tackling** every stage of your operation and **meeting the demands of** every company involved in what, we must all agree, is a major initiative.

A. Was ERGO Ihnen anbietet, ist eine **Zusammenarbeit von Anfang an**, wobei wir Sie auf jeder Stufe unterstützen. Wir haben **eine breite Palette** von Programmen, von denen jedes in der Lage ist, mit jeder Entwicklungsstufe Ihrer Operation **fertig zu werden** und **die Anforderungen** jedes Unternehmens **zu erfüllen** - was, wie wir

T. So how do you propose doing that?

A. I read your promotional material with interest. It is very comprehensive and informative. What I am proposing is that you expand your **dossier** now with our **brochure material**.

T. But I'm giving you exclusivity in that case.

A. Not necessarily. ERGO is **well aware** there are other software companies out there. We don't want to lock them out of this particular market. ERGO just believes that no other company has organized its large variety of products to **suit the** kind of **purpose** associated with a **venture** like yours.

T. Wait, wait. You're leaving me behind …

uns wohl alle einig sind, ein Hauptanliegen sein muss.

T. Und wie wollen Sie das bewerkstelligen?

A. Ich habe Ihr Promotionmaterial mit Interesse gelesen. Es ist sehr umfassend und informativ. Was ich Ihnen anbiete ist, dass Sie Ihr **Dossier** jetzt um unsere **Broschüren** erweitern.

T. Aber damit würde ich Ihnen exklusive Privilegien einräumen.

A. Nicht unbedingt. ERGO ist sich **wohl bewusst**, dass es da draußen auch andere Softwarefirmen gibt. Wir wollen sie von diesem speziellen Markt nicht ausschließen. ERGO ist nur der Meinung, dass kein anderes Unternehmen sein umfassendes Angebot an Produkten so organisiert hat, dass sie **den Anforderungen entsprechen**, die eine **Unternehmung** wie die Ihre mit sich bringt.

T. Warten Sie, warten Sie. Da komme ich nicht mit …

Background Information

Angus proposes ERGO Ltd **coming in on the ground floor** meaning **being involved at the initial stages**, another expression with »ground« to add to those learnt in the previous section of the dialogue.

Angus seemed to be very **well-versed** in Cyber-Parks's operations meaning **he knows a lot about it**. One could also say he is well-informed, which has a similar meaning.
»**Well-versed**« and »**well-informed**« are both **compound adjectives** formed from the adverb »well« (from »good«), and the past participle. They are usually hyphenated (-).
Here are some more examples:

well-established	existing for a long time
well-advised	careful, prudent
well-appointed	having all the necessary equipment, furniture, etc.
well-connected	friendly with or related to rich or influential people
well-timed	done or said at the right time
well-disposed (towards somebody)	sympathetic or friendly
well-thought-of	respected or liked

Train Yourself

Suchen Sie nun für die folgenden Sätze das richtige zusammengesetzte Adjektiv!

1. Being ▬▬▬▬▬▬▬▬▬ and having the right contacts is a great advantage to getting ahead in life.
2. The Marketing Manager was very ▬▬▬▬▬▬▬▬▬ in the company and everybody wished him well on his retirement.
3. The offer to take over the company was ▬▬▬▬▬▬▬▬▬ as just a week earlier it had been on the verge of bankruptcy.

4. The company was very ▓▓▓▓▓▓▓▓▓▓▓▓▓▓▓▓ and had been in existence for more than 200 years.
5. One would be ▓▓▓▓▓▓▓▓▓▓▓▓▓▓▓▓ to be thoroughly familiar with a client's background before attempting a sale.
6. The new office was ▓▓▓▓▓▓▓▓▓▓▓▓▓▓▓▓ and in a very desirable location.
7. Gordon was ▓▓▓▓▓▓▓▓▓▓▓▓▓▓▓▓ in every area of the company's operations and subsequently was offered the job.
8. I'm not particularly ▓▓▓▓▓▓▓▓▓▓▓▓▓▓▓▓ towards anybody who can't do their job properly.

Talk Talk Talk

(Some two hours later)

T. I think we can break there for lunch. It will give me the opportunity to put the questions that have raised themselves in my mind ...

(At lunch)

T. I liked your proposal, Mr Fairbairn - may I call you Angus? Please call me Alistair. But what worries me a little is the **servicing guarantees** you have to offer. There's no doubt that the **package** you have put together is a good one. In fact, I don't think it could be **bettered**. But we have a responsibility to our clients, the companies who will be setting up operations here. If we recommend your package and then if ERGO **falls down on its promises we are**

(Ungefähr zwei Stunden später)

T. Ich glaube, wir können jetzt Mittagspause einlegen. Dabei habe ich Gelegenheit, die Fragen zu stellen, die mir in den Kopf geschossen sind ...

(Beim Mittagessen)

T. Ihr Angebot hat mir gefallen, Mr. Fairbairn - darf ich Sie Angus nennen? Bitte nennen Sie mich Alistair. Was mir ein bisschen Sorgen macht, sind die **Service-Garantien**, die Sie zu bieten haben. Ich habe keinen Zweifel daran, dass das **Service-Paket**, das Sie zusammengestellt haben, gut ist. Ich glaube sogar, dass es gar nicht **besser sein** könnte. Aber wir haben eine Verantwortung gegenüber unseren Kunden, den Unternehmen die hier Geschäfte

first in the firing line. How are we to be protected?

S. May I answer this one, Angus? ERGO's **payment plan** includes insurance from one of Britain's leading companies. Our package also has the support of two major banks, which means **payment can be spread out** over a period of up to five years, a kind of leasing, if you like. You are of course aware that big tax breaks are available for the involvement of companies such as ours – not to speak of subsidies. But, of course, that's your territory.

T. Quite right! We have gone fully into all **funding questions** and **are satisfied on that score**. But, please, don't let your meal go cold. That roast beef is best Aberdeen Angus!

machen werden. Wenn wir Ihr Paket empfehlen und ERGO dann **seinen Versprechungen nicht nachkommt, werden wir als Erstes gefeuert**. Wir können wir uns davor schützen?

S. Darf ich die Frage beantworten, Angus?
ERGO's **Finanzplan** beinhaltet die Versicherung durch eines unserer führenden britischen Unternehmen. Unser Paket wird auch von zwei großen Banken unterstützt, was einen **Zahlungszeitraum** von bis zu fünf Jahren zulässt - eine Art Leasing, wenn Sie so wollen. Sie wissen sicher, dass es bedeutende Steuererleichterungen für Unternehmen wie unseres gibt – ganz zu schweigen von Subventionen. Aber das ist natürlich Ihr Fachgebiet.

T. Sie haben Recht! Wir sind alle **Basisfragen** durchgegangen und **sind bis jetzt zufrieden**. Aber bitte, lassen Sie Ihr Essen nicht kalt werden. Das Roastbeef ist bestes Angus-Rind aus Aberdeen!

Background Information

In the last section we looked at compound adjectives formed from adverbs. In this section there is an example of a very common **adverb being used as a verb**, i.e. **better**. Mr Travis says that ERGO **couldn't be bettered**, in other words it **couldn't be improved**.

The second language point concerns the use of »**score**«. This word is more often associated with **sports**, e.g. scoring a goal in football or a try in rugby. Alistair Travis, however, says that he is **satisfied on that score** (i.e. with the question of funding). »**On that score**« means »**in that regard**« or »**as far as that is concerned.**« A »**score**« also means **twenty** e.g. »There were three score and ten at the party«, i.e. 70, although this usage is now very old-fashioned. More commonly we say »**scores**« to mean **many**, e.g. »There were scores of people at the match! I couldn't believe it.«

Below are some more common expressions with »**score**« and »**better**«.

to know the score	to know everything about the situation
to get the better of	to win a victory over somebody
to go one better	to improve on a previous success
to have seen better days	to be in a worse condition than it used to be
for better or worse	whether one likes it or not
to think better of	to decide not to do something

Train Yourself

Verwenden Sie die Wendungen in der folgenden Übung!

1. We were going to invest in a computer training scheme before we discovered how much it would cost and then ▬▬▬▬▬▬▬▬▬▬▬▬▬▬▬▬▬▬▬ it.
2. My car ▬▬▬▬▬▬▬▬▬▬▬▬. Shall we take yours to Scotland?
3. Although sales in the last quarter were impressive the CEO wants us to ▬▬▬▬▬▬▬▬▬▬▬▬▬▬▬▬ and achieve the highest sales figures in the company's history.
4. You can trust James with the account, he ▬▬▬▬▬▬▬▬▬▬▬▬▬▬▬▬.
5. ▬▬▬▬▬▬▬▬▬▬▬▬▬▬▬ if the staff ask for salary increases we are going to have to listen to them.
6. I've never seen so many delegates as there were at last week's conference. There were ▬▬▬▬▬▬▬▬▬▬▬▬▬▬▬▬▬ of them!

7. Peter is the top salesman in the company nobody can ▓▓▓▓▓▓▓▓▓▓▓▓▓▓▓▓▓▓▓▓▓▓ him.
8. The company finally ▓▓▓▓▓▓▓▓▓▓▓▓▓▓▓▓▓▓▓▓▓▓ their main rival and succeeded in winning the contract.

 **Talk Talk Talk**

(Travis's office, the next day. Steve, Peter and Angus enter)

T. Good morning, gentlemen! Sleep well, I trust?

S. Very well, thank you Alistair. That Scottish beer knocked me out for the night. And the way they serve it – in jugs. Not like in England. I have difficulty there getting a proper pint.

T. (laughs) It's another example of our Scottish way with money. You get more beer and pay less!

S. I noticed that – and so does my head this morning. Not to worry! Let's get down to business.

T. I have invited the **Chief Executive** of one of our interested enterprises to join in the talks. You'll get an idea then of the kind of concerns **facing** these small com-

(Am nächsten Tag in Travis Büro. Steve, Peter und Angus treten ein)

T. Guten Morgen, meine Herren! Nehme an, Sie haben gut geschlafen?

S. Sehr gut, ich danke Ihnen, Alistair. Das schottische Bier hat mich für einen Abend ins Aus befördert. Und wie es serviert wird – in Krügen. Nicht wie in England. Dort habe ich Schwierigkeiten, ein ordentliches Pint zu bekommen.

T. (lacht) Noch ein Beispiel für unsere schottische Art, mit Geld umzugehen. Man bekommt mehr Bier und zahlt weniger!

S. Das habe ich gemerkt – und mein Kopf auch heute morgen. Aber keine Sorge! Lassen Sie uns zum Geschäft kommen.

T. Ich habe den **Hauptgeschäftsführer** von einem der interessierten Unternehmen mit zum Gespräch eingeladen. Dann bekommen Sie einen Eindruck von

panies in the new, electronic market place.

der Art der Bedenken, die diese kleinen Unternehmen auf dem neuen, elektronischen Weltmarkt **haben**.

S. We'll be most interested to meet him.

S. Wir sind sehr gespannt darauf, ihn kennen zu lernen.

T. Actually, it's a »she«! A very clever young woman who has **put** her fashion business **on-line** – even offers **on-line fashion parades**. You'll see.

T. Es ist übrigens eine »Sie«. Eine sehr kluge junge Frau, die mit ihrem Modegeschäft **online ist** - sogar **Online-Modeschauen** anbietet. Sie werden sehen.

S. Fascinating.

S. Faszinierend.

(The Telephone rings)

(Das Telefon klingelt)

T. That'll be her now ...

T. Das wird sie sein...

Background Information

Mr Travis in this section of the dialogue talks about the problems **facing** small companies in the electronic market place meaning the problems »**requiring attention**«.
»**To face up to something**« has the similar meaning of **accepting or dealing with something unpleasant**. A common expression is »**to face the facts**«, implying that the person involved **must deal with reality rather than trying to avoid it**.
Let's look at some more »**face**« expressions:

face the music	to deal with the difficulties or consequences of one's actions
face value	as sth. appears to be initially
a long face	a serious or unhappy expression on somebody's face
staring s.o. in the face	be obvious or clearly in view

to lose face	to lose the respect or good opinion of others
to show one's face	to appear or present oneself
to talk till someone is blue in the face	to talk endlessly without achieving the desired result
to have egg on one's face	to look stupid or foolish

Train Yourself

Füllen Sie die Lücken mit diesen Wendungen!

1. How was your meeting with Jarvis yesterday?
   A waste of time. I ▒▒▒▒ and got absolutely nowhere.
2. You shouldn't take things ▒▒▒▒ without having thought about them first.
3. Disaster was ▒▒▒▒ us ▒▒▒▒ until Tony came up with a masterplan to save the company.
4. When the Chief Executive came into the meeting with ▒▒▒▒ we all knew something was wrong.
5. Graham lost one of the company's most valued clients and is now on his way to head office to ▒▒▒▒.
6. I really had ▒▒▒▒ when I turned up to a sales meeting in Cardiff and found out it was actually being held in Swansea.
7. Are you going to the staff Christmas party?
   Oh, I'll ▒▒▒▒ for an hour or so but I need to have an early night tonight.
8. We've got to ▒▒▒▒, unless we become more consumer friendly profits will continue to go down.
9. When dealing with Asian clients one must be aware that on no account can they be seen to ▒▒▒▒. This is very important in Asian societies.

Talk Talk Talk

(Still at the office)

T. Good morning, Miss Sinclair. How nice to meet you again! (He introduces Steve, Peter and Angus to Bettina Sinclair)

B. I'm very interested in meeting you. It's actually the first time I've met practically the whole **executive and sales staff of a company** we want to do business with.

S. I just hope we have the necessary experience to **handle** a company such as yours. Fashion is not our **strong point**.

A. What Steve is trying to say is that we usually deal with companies of a lower market profile than yours. Fashion is an extremely **consumer-oriented area of business**.

B. Not necessarily. We are a **retail outlet** primarily, that's true. But we have struck very **productive** and **lucrative deals** with larger fashion firms. We aim exclusively at the upper end of the market.

(Immer noch im Büro)

T. Guten Morgen, Miss Sinclair. Wie schön, Sie wiederzusehen! (Er stellt Steve, Peter und Angus Bettina Sinclair vor)

B. Ich freue mich sehr, Sie kennen zu lernen. Es ist tatsächlich das erste Mal, dass ich quasi **die gesamte Geschäftsführung und den Verkaufsstab eines Unternehmens** treffe, mit denen wir Geschäfte machen möchten.

S. Ich hoffe nur, wir haben die nötige Erfahrung, um mit einem Unternehmen wie Ihrem **umzugehen**. Mode ist nicht unsere **stärkste Seite**.

A. Was Steve sagen will ist, dass wir für gewöhnlich mit Firmen zusammenarbeiten, die ein niedrigeres Marktprofil haben als Ihres. Mode ist ein extrem **konsumentenorientiertes Geschäftsgebiet**.

B. Nicht unbedingt. Es stimmt, wir sind in erster Linie eine **Einzelhandels-Niederlassung**. Aber wir haben uns sehr **produktive** und **lukrative Geschäfte** mit größeren Modefirmen erkämpft. Wir wollen

P. But how can you do that online? Surely your customers need the personal touch – the experience of actually attending one of your fashion shows.

P. Aber wie können Sie das online realisieren? Sicher brauchen Ihre Kunden den persönlichen Kontakt – die Erfahrung, wirklich bei einer Ihrer Modenschauen anwesend zu sein.

unbedingt an das obere Ende des Marktsegmentes vorstoßen.

B. That's true to a certain extent. And the one aspect of the business doesn't exclude the other. Let me explain ...

B. Das stimmt bis zu einem gewissen Grad. Und der eine Aspekt des Geschäftes schließt den anderen nicht aus. Lassen Sie mich das erklären ...

Background Information

Steve tells Bettina that fashion is not ERGO's **strong point**, meaning that it's not the **strongest feature or aspect** of the company. »**The point**« can mean the essential thing, the principal idea. So when a listener feels that a speaker is not dealing with the matter at hand, he can say »**That's not the point**« or »**What point are you trying to make?**«

Let's look at some common expressions with »**point**«:

to point out	to draw attention to a fact
to make a point of	to make sure that one does something or emphasizes something
to take someone's point	to understand or accept what somebody is saying
in point of fact	in reality, actually
beside the point	not directly concerned with the main point of a discussion
on the point of	about to (do something)
not to put too fine a point on it	to speak plainly and honestly
to point a finger	to blame/accuse somebody

Train Yourself

Verwenden Sie die Begriffe in der nun folgenden Übung!

1. The Sales Director was ▓▓▓▓▓▓▓▓▓▓ hiring the new salesperson when he changed his mind on receiving an unsatisfactory reference from his previous employer.
2. No-one's ▓▓▓▓▓▓▓▓▓▓ here but we must face the facts; our performance has not been good enough.
3. I ▓▓▓▓▓▓▓▓▓▓ writing all my appointments down in my diary just in case one of them slips my mind.
4. Excuse me. I ▓▓▓▓▓▓▓▓▓▓ about the need to be more cost-effective but surely, staff reductions are not the answer ...
5. We had planned to stay overnight in the Britannia Hotel but Peter ▓▓▓▓▓▓▓▓▓▓ that it would be quicker to take the overnight train instead.
6. ▓▓▓▓▓▓▓▓▓▓ Neil, your work here has not been up to standard and this is why I am asking for your resignation.
7. Microsoft is not just an enormously profitable company; ▓▓▓▓▓▓▓▓▓▓ it is the most lucrative in the world.
8. When it comes to making an impression on a potential customer the regional dialect of the salesperson is ▓▓▓▓▓▓▓▓▓▓. It is the personality that matters.

 Talk Talk Talk

(Two hours later)

S. Miss Sinclair, that was a **fascinating account** of an **area of business** which is entirely new to us. Now tell us how ERGO can help you.

B. I understand you have a program which I think could have

(Zwei Stunden später)

S. Miss Sinclair, das war eine **faszinierende Einführung** in ein **Geschäftsgebiet**, das völlig neu für uns ist. Sagen Sie mir, wie ERGO Ihnen helfen kann.

B. Soweit ich weiß, haben Sie ein Programm, dass wie ich glaube **für**

been **tailored to our needs** - this **electronic accounting system**. I'm a **small operation**, basically a **one-person show**. I can't afford a proper **accounting staff**, although business is **increasing at an encouraging rate**. Doing **business on-line** can be extremely labour intensive. I must tell you that I have made inquiries with other companies such as yours, but one of the things I have learnt from business is compare, compare, compare – until you've run out of **comparison possibilities**.

unsere Bedürfnisse wie geschaffen ist - dieses **elektronische Buchungssystem**. Ich bin eine **kleine Geschäftseinheit**, eigentlich ein **Ein-Personen-Unternehmen**. Ich kann mir kein richtiges **Buchführungs-Personal** leisten, auch wenn das Geschäft **eine zunehmende Erfolgsrate aufweist**. **Online-Geschäfte** können sehr arbeitsintensiv sein. Ich muss sagen, ich habe Erkundigungen bei anderen Firmen eingezogen, denn eines der Dinge, die ich im Geschäft gelernt habe ist: vergleichen, vergleichen, vergleichen – bis einem die **Vergleichsmöglichkeiten** ausgehen.

S. Very Scottish, if I may say, Miss Sinclair. But now it's over to you, Angus.

S. Sehr schottisch, wenn ich so sagen darf, Miss Sinclair. Aber jetzt zu Ihnen, Angus.

A. Let me first of all give you all the literature we have on the program. I sent you an **introductory pamphlet**, which I hoped would arouse your interest. It has I see. Now my second proposal is that you inform yourself fully about our **accounting program** and that we meet over lunch tomorrow to discuss the system further. My third proposal is that we visit your office to show you the program at work – I'm sure you'll be impressed.

A. Lassen Sie mich Ihnen zu allererst die Literatur geben, die wir über dieses Programm haben. Ich hatte Ihnen eine **kurze Einführung** geschickt, von der ich hoffte, Sie würde Ihr Interesse wecken. Wie ich sehe, hat sie das getan. Mein zweites Angebot besteht darin, dass Sie sich selbst vollständig über unser **Abrechnungssystem** informieren und dass wir uns morgen zum Mittagessen treffen und das System weiter diskutieren. Mein drittes Angebot ist, dass wir zu

Ihnen ins Büro kommen und Ihnen das Programm im Einsatz zeigen – ich bin sicher, Sie werden beeindruckt sein.

B. That's fine by me. But you'll have a bit of a journey – I work from home in the Highlands. In this business, as you know, **you can work from anywhere**. My office has a wonderful view of the mountains – something I can't enjoy in Glasgow.

B. Von mir aus gerne. Aber Sie haben eine etwas weitere Reise vor sich – ich arbeite von meinem Zuhause im Hochland aus. In diesem Geschäft **können Sie**, wie Sie wissen, **von überall aus arbeiten**. Mein Büro verfügt über einen wunderbaren Blick auf die Berge – etwas, das ich in Glasgow nicht genießen kann.

S. You're very lucky. Can't ERGO follow that example, Peter?

S. Sie haben Glück. Kann ERGO das nicht auch machen, Peter?

P. If it did, I might find myself back in Hamburg – just when I'm getting to know and like London.

P. Wenn ERGO das täte, würde ich mich in Hamburg wiederfinden – und das gerade jetzt, wo ich London kennen und lieben gelernt habe.

A. **Give me** the Highlands.

A. **Auf in** die Highlands.

 **Train Yourself**

1. Steve macht Miss Sinclair zwei Vorschläge: »Now my second proposal is that you inform yourself fully about our accounting program and that we meet over lunch tomorrow to discuss the system further. My third proposal is that we visit your office to show you the program at work.« Es handelt sich hier um eine indirekte Form der Aufforderung.

Seien Sie direkter und formen Sie die Sätze entsprechend um!

2. Finden Sie die richtigen Begriffe!

a. a small booklet of information   ....

b. a body of persons employed in an establishment, usually on management, administration, clerical, etc. work as distinct from manual   ....

c. a descriptive report   ....

d. an agency   ....

e. the sale directly to the consumer or in small quantities   ....

operation, retail, pamphlet, staff, account.

 Vocabulary

a broad palette	eine breite Palette
accounting system	Buchhaltungssystem
an important catch	ein wichtiger Fang
beforehand	im Voraus
to better	verbessern
to break	unterbrechen
broadband communications	Breitband-Kommunikation
chief executive	Hauptgeschäftsführer
to come in on the ground floor	von Anfang an zusammenarbeiten
consumer-orientated	konsumentenorientiert

deal	Geschäft; Angebot
devolution	Dezentralisierung .
Down to business.	Kommen wir zum Geschäftlichen.
to fall down on s.o.'s promises	jds. Versprechungen nicht nachkommen
to get sth. off the ground	etw. in Gang bringen
to handle	umgehen mit
How's business?	Wie gehen die Geschäfte?
to increase at an encouraging rate	hohe Zuwachsraten verzeichnen
introductory pamphlet	kurze Einführung
lucrative	lukrativ
to make a big bid	sich sehr bemühen
to make straight for	sich sofort aufmachen zu
to meet the demands of	die Anforderungen erfüllen
new revolution	neue Revolution
payment plan	Finanzplan
to provide	bereitstellen
to put on file	abspeichern
retail outlet	Einzelhandels-Niederlassung
sales chief	Verkaufsleiter
to set up	sich niederlassen
strong point	starke Seite
subsidies	Subventionen
to suit the purpose	den Anforderungen entsprechen
to tackle sth.	fertig werden mit etw.
tailored	maßgeschneidert
tax breaks	Steuererleichterungen
venture	Unternehmung
well aware	im Klaren darüber

Settle conditions of a contract
Vertragsbedingungen aushandeln

 **Here we go**

Immer noch in Glasgow ist Peter fasziniert von den Möglichkeiten, die die neuen Internet-Verkaufsseiten eröffnen. Aber auch Kunden aus traditionellen Branchen, wie zum Beispiel Theaterdarsteller und ihre Agenten, haben mittlerweile Bedarf an Softwareprogrammen, um Ihre Daten modern verwalten zu können. Hamilton McDonald, der Partner von Angus in Edinburgh, ist gerade dabei, ein Geschäft in diesem Bereich abzuschließen und lässt Peter und Steve daran teilhaben, was die beiden hochinteressant finden; aber was Peter noch viel mehr interessiert, ist Melissa's unerwartete Anwesenheit in Edinburgh und der Grund für ihren Aufenthalt …

 Talk Talk Talk

(Glasgow hotel. Breakfast room)

S. Well, that was one heck of an interesting excursion to the Highlands. It's remarkable how that young woman can operate so successfully from home.

A. Modern technology. **Electronic commerce**. You can do business now from just anywhere – a pal of mine has a holiday home on the Isle of Mull and operates mostly from there.

(Das Hotel in Glasgow. Im Frühstücksraum)

S. Tja, das war ein ziemlich interessanter Ausflug in die Highlands. Schon erstaunlich, wie erfolgreich eine junge Frau von zu Hause aus arbeiten kann.

A. Moderne Technologie. **Elektronischer Handel**. Man kann sein Geschäft von überall aus betreiben – ein Freund von mir hat ein Ferienhaus auf der *Isle of Mull* und arbeitet hauptsächlich von dort aus.

P. I've read several reports on these so-called »**cyber ports**« which are **springing up all over the place**. It's a really interesting development. At the time of the industrial revolution one hundred years or so ago **centres of business activity** grew around main **thoroughfares**, rivers and harbours. Glasgow is an example. In the **high-tech age** these **business centres** are being created at geographical locations where telecommunications are good and **a highly-qualified pool of labour** exists.

P. Ich habe schon mehrere Berichte über diese so genannten »Cyber Ports« gelesen, die jetzt **überall aus dem Boden schießen**. Eine wirklich interessante Entwicklung. Vor etwa hundert Jahren, zurzeit der industriellen Revolution erwuchsen die **Handelszentren** an **Hauptverkehrsstraßen** an Flüssen und Häfen. Glasgow ist ein Beispiel dafür. Im **Zeitalter der Hochtechnologie** werden solche **Handelszentren** an geographischen Punkten errichtet, an denen die Telekommunikationsstruktur gut errichtet ist und wo **genügend hochqualifizierte Mitarbeiter** zu finden sind.

S. It's a very interesting development, I agree, Peter. But I'll have to have another pair of kippers before I can really **tune in to** this level of conversation …

S. Eine sehr interessante Entwicklung, Peter, da stimme ich Ihnen zu. Aber ich brauche noch so ein paar *Kippers* – Bücklinge – bevor ich dieser Ebene der Konversation **folgen** kann …

Background Information

1. So-called »**cyber-ports**« are now being created throughout the world. They are an officially planned and organised version of the »Silicon Valley« IT (Information Technology) developments which have arisen almost spontaneously in California, southern France and, of course, in Germany (around Munich and in Baden-Wuerttemberg). Asia is a leader in this field, and »**cyber-ports**« are taking shape in Hong Kong, Singapore, Malaysia, Thailand and even in India (Bangalore).

2. Steve says to Peter that he'll have to have another pair of kippers before **tuning in to** Peter's conversation. »**To tune in**« means **to concentrate**. »**To have to do something**« means that **the person is obliged to do it** and in this example Steve is using the future form with »**will**«. Let's look at how this verb changes depending on the verbal tense:

Present Simple	have to (»must« is also possible here)
Past Simple	had to
Will-Future	will have to (*or* 'll have to)
Going to-Future	am/is/are going to have + infinitive
Past Perfect	had had to (*or* 'd had to)
Present Perfect	have had to ('ve had to)
Would/Could/May/Should/Might	+ have to

Note: although »**must**« and »**have to**« possess almost identical meanings, in the negative their meanings differ. »I don't have to speak French«, implies an absence of obligation, i.e. »I can if I want to but it's not obligatory«. »I mustn't speak French«, however, implies prohibition and is the same as »I can't speak French even though I want to« or »I'm not allowed to.«

 Train Yourself

Verwenden Sie in den folgenden Sätzen die jeweils richtige Form von »to have to«:

1. I don't know what's happening tomorrow, we ▓▓▓▓▓▓▓▓▓▓▓▓ get there early but I'll ring you tonight to confirm the time.
2. If you go to this business fair on the 24th you ▓▓▓▓▓▓▓▓▓▓ report back to us on any areas of interest, OK?
3. We ▓▓▓▓▓▓▓▓▓▓ keep ahead of any important developments in the marketplace.

4. Since the company relocated to a new site Helen _____ live in a hotel.
5. Hello John, listen, I _____ speak with you about a matter of the utmost urgency.
6. By the time the new computer arrived she _____ to use the one in the office for two months.
7. All the candidates _____ take an entrance exam first. If we did this the overall standard would be much higher.
8. The company _____ have a complete overhaul of the computer systems when they crashed the day before.
9. We're _____ work all weekend to get this work done by Monday.
10. If your performance doesn't improve I _____ speak to the Managing Director.

 Talk Talk Talk

P. What **intrigues me**, Angus, is how a **sales team** operates in this new environment. Don't you have to adopt a whole new **strategy**? You can hardly go knocking on doors in a **virtual marketplace**, can you?

A. Well, we saw yesterday that even the **virtual marketplace** doesn't make the tried and tested **personal approach** superfluous. A face behind the product will always be a central factor of successful selling. But, you're right, the **IT revolution** – if I can call it that – has added a new dimension to selling. Every company, large and small, now has a **website**. It's a necessity. Without it you can't

P. Was **mich besonders interessiert**, Angus, ist, wie ein **Verkaufsteam** in dieser neuen Umgebung überhaupt arbeitet. Muss man dazu nicht eine völlig neue **Strategie** entwickeln? Man kann an einem **virtuellen Markt** ja wohl kaum einfach an die Tür klopfen, oder?

A. Tja, wir haben ja gestern selbst gesehen, dass selbst ein **virtueller Markt** den altbewährten **persönlichen Ansatz** nicht überflüssig macht. Das Gesicht hinter dem Produkt wird immer ein zentraler Faktor des erfolgreichen Verkaufens sein. Aber Sie haben Recht, die **IT-Revolution** – wenn ich es mal so nennen darf – hat dem Verkaufsgeschäft eine völlig neue Dimension gegeben. Jede Firma,

operate in this new marketplace. Just as we used to have to attend very closely to the content and **visual presentation** of our **marketing material – brochures** and the like – we now have to design, or have designed, a website that is also attractive, informative and **easily accessible**. ERGO is a good example. Whoever drew up our website knew what he or she was doing.

S. Melissa oversaw it.

A. Clever girl that. But I hear she might be moving …

P. What? Where?

A. The **grapevine** extends even to Scotland. **Word** reached me from Edinburgh …

S. Edinburgh! Look at the time. We've got to **get on the road** – we have to be there by 12.

egal ob groß oder klein, hat heute ihre **Website**. Das ist unumgänglich. Ohne diese kann man auf diesem neuen Absatzmarkt gar nicht aktiv werden. Genau so wie wir uns sehr sorgsam um die **visuelle Präsentation** unseres **Marketing-Materials** kümmern müssen – etwa in Form von **Broschüren** – müssen wir nun auch eine Website designen oder designen lassen, die genau so attraktiv, informativ und **leicht zugänglich** ist. ERGO ist ein gutes Beispiel dafür. Wer immer unsere Website entworfen hat, wusste, was er oder sie tat.

S. Melissa hatte die Gesamtleitung darüber.

A. Ein cleveres Mädchen. Aber ich habe gehört, dass sie vielleicht wechselt …

P. Was? Wohin?

A. Die **Gerüchteküche** reicht selbst bis Schottland. Ich habe ein **Gerücht** aus Edinburgh gehört …

S. Edinburgh! Es ist schon spät! Wir müssen uns **auf den Weg machen** – wir müssen um 12 dort sein.

Background Information

»**We've got to get on the road**« announces Steve when he realises they're running behind time. **Get**, in this context, means **to arrive**, e.g. »We have to get to Edinburgh by 12«.

This very common word can also be used to mean: **to become**, e.g. »I'm getting tired of this«; **to bring**, e.g. »Can you get me this file, please?«; **to buy**, e.g. »I got some great things in the shops yesterday«; **to receive**, e.g. »I got an e-mail from the Accounts Department«; **to obtain/achieve**, e.g. »I got my diploma last year in IT«; and **to catch**, e.g., »We got the train just on time«, amongst others!

»**Get**« is also used as a part of several »phrasal verbs«. Some are listed below:

to get over	to recover
to get by	to manage or to survive
to get through to	to establish contact
to get something over with	to come to the end of something
to get round to	to find time to do something
to get on	to make progress
to get together	to have a meeting or party
to get away with	to do something wrong without being caught or punished

Train Yourself

Verwenden Sie die oben stehenden »phrasal verbs« in der folgenden Übung!

1. Hello Frank! Len here. Listen, let's ▒▒▒▒▒▒▒▒ some time this week and go over the Johnson account. Then we can have a drink afterwards. What do you say?
2. How are you ▒▒▒▒▒▒▒▒ with your new life in Britain, Peter?

3. I'm busy right now but hopefully I'll ▓▓▓▓▓▓ to doing it next week. Is that OK?
4. I've been calling Steve all day and I still can't ▓▓▓▓▓ him.
5. Some companies use offshore accounts to ▓▓▓▓▓ paying less tax.
6. During the recession the company ▓▓▓▓▓ through a reduction of overheads and a reduced workforce.
7. It took Tony a long time to ▓▓▓▓▓ the shock of being made redundant.
8. I wasn't looking forward to doing the company accounts but I decided to start straight away and ▓▓▓▓▓ it ▓▓▓▓▓.

 Talk Talk Talk

(In the car, on the drive to Edinburgh)

S. In Edinburgh, we'll be meeting Angus's **sidekick**, Hamilton McDonald. If you think Angus is your true Scot, you wait till you meet Hamilton. He's such a nationalist that he thinks working for a **London-based** company is treason. But he likes the money! Isn't that so, Angus?

A. You said it, Steve!

P. He's obviously successful?

S. Hamilton's so successful he could even sell you – what do you

(Im Wagen, auf der Fahrt nach Edinburgh)

S. In Edinburgh treffen wir Angus' **Partner**, Hamilton McDonald. Wenn Sie glauben, dass Angus schon ein echter Schotte ist, dann warten Sie, bis Sie Hamilton kennen lernen. Er ist so ein Nationalist, dass er es schon für Verrat hält, für eine Firma zu arbeiten, die ihren **Hauptsitz in London** hat. Aber ihn lockt das Geld! Ist es nicht so, Angus?

A. Sie sagen es, Steve!

P. Er ist also offensichtlich erfolgreich?

S. Hamilton ist so erfolgreich, er könnte Ihnen sogar – was isst man

eat out there in place of kippers? Matties?

bei euch an Stelle von *Kippers*? »Matties«? – ja, »Matties« verkaufen.

P. Matjes, Steve. Matjes.

P. Matjes, Steve. Matjes.

S. Don't know how you can get your tongue around that language of yours, Peter, my friend. But Hamilton would and he'd **end up** exporting Matjes to Hamburg. Hamilton's his name – but I call him **ham** for short. In fact, he really is something of an actor – the marketplace is his personal stage.

S. Ich weiß nicht, ob ich meine Zunge je dazu bringen kann, eure Sprache zu sprechen, Peter, mein Freund. Aber Hamilton **könnte** es und **am Ende** würde er Matjes nach Hamburg exportieren. Er heißt zwar Hamilton – aber ich nenne ihn »**ham**« – **einen Schmierenkomödianten**. Er ist in der Tat etwas wie ein Schauspieler – der Markt ist seine private Bühne.

P. I can't wait to meet him.

P. Ich kann es gar nicht abwarten, ihn kennen zu lernen.

S. You'll need some preparation. Let's **pull in** here for a coffee. And drink it the local way – with a **dram of** whisky …

S. Sie müssen darauf vorbereitet werden. Lassen Sie uns für einen Kaffee **anhalten**. Wir trinken ihn auf die für die Gegend übliche Weise – mit einem **Schuss** Whisky …

Background Information

Steve suggests that they **pull in** for a coffee, meaning **to park** or **stop the car**. One can also say »**pull up**«, e.g. »Let's pull up over there.«. There are several other phrasal verbs with »**pull**«, including »**to pull out**« which means **to start the car moving** and is the opposite of **pull in/up**. Other ones are listed below:

to pull off	to manage, to succeed
to pull out all the stops	to use all one's energy and effort
to pull in one's belt	to spend less money
to pull one's socks up	to make a serious effort to improve one's behaviour or work
to pull someone's leg	to make fun of a person in a friendly way
to pull the carpet out from under someone's feet	to stop giving help or support without any warning
to pull one's weight	to take one's fair share of the work

 Train Yourself

Verwenden Sie die »phrasal verbs« mit »pull« in der unten stehenden Übung:

1. Unless Trevor ▒▒▒▒▒▒▒▒▒▒ he could find himself out of a job.
2. The slump in the company's fortunes seems to have been a result of people not ▒▒▒▒▒▒▒▒▒ their ▒▒▒▒▒▒▒▒▒.
3. Bob is known as the joker in the office, he's always ▒▒▒▒▒▒▒▒▒ people's ▒▒▒▒▒▒▒▒▒
4. We (a) ▒▒▒▒▒▒▒▒▒ of the motorway service-station at 2 o'clock and then had to (b) ▒▒▒▒▒▒▒▒▒ again when we realized we were short of petrol.
5. The sales team have ▒▒▒▒▒▒▒▒▒ it ▒▒▒▒▒▒▒▒▒! The new contract is worth millions to the company.
6. At the meeting the Chief Executive told the staff that they would have to ▒▒▒▒▒▒▒▒▒ their ▒▒▒▒▒▒▒▒▒ and wait until next year for a salary raise.
7. The bank ▒▒▒▒▒▒▒▒▒ our ▒▒▒▒▒▒▒▒▒ when they refused to give us any more credit.
8. We ▒▒▒▒▒▒▒▒▒ and worked through the night but the deal still fell through.

 **Talk Talk Talk**

(Glasgow)

A. Here we are. Hamilton's office. You can park right outside ... Good morning, we're here to see Mr McDonald. **Is he in?**

Receptionist: A very good morning to you all. He certainly is in. Shall I call him for you?

A. Be a good woman and do that for us, if you please ...

Receptionist: He's expecting you. I'll take you up to his office ...

H. Good morning, Angus! How are you doing? I haven't seen you in months. You must be busy.

A. I've had a busy time lately, that's true. Right now I'm **showing my two colleagues from London around** – Steve Blackman and Peter Brückner.

H. How do you do! Welcome to Scotland. We've only had **contact on the phone**, Mr Blackman – Steve isn't it? But I don't know Mr Brückner.

(Glasgow)

A. Da wären wir. Hamiltons Büro. Sie können direkt davor parken ... Guten Morgen, wir möchten gern zu Mr. McDonald. **Ist er da?**

Empfangsdame: Einen schönen guten Morgen zusammen. Natürlich ist er da. Soll ich ihm Bescheid sagen?

A. Seien Sie so gut und machen Sie das für uns ...

Empfangsdame: Er erwartet sie. Ich werde Sie zu seinem Büro führen ...

H. Guten Morgen, Angus! Wie geht es Ihnen? Wir haben uns seit Monaten nicht gesehen. Sie müssen ja ziemlich beschäftigt sein.

A. Ich hatte in letzter Zeit wirklich viel zu tun, das stimmt. Im Augenblick **führe** ich gerade zwei Kollegen aus London **herum** – Steve Blackman und Peter Brückner.

H. Wie geht es Ihnen? Willkommen in Schottland. Wir haben schon einmal **telefoniert**, Mr. Blackman – Steve, nicht wahr? Aber Mr. Brückner kenne ich noch nicht.

S. Our new Assistant Managing Director.

H. Oh, I'd better **watch my way**, then, hadn't I?

S. Don't worry, Hamilton. I've filled Peter in on the way from Glasgow – I told him you're one of our best but also one of our most theatrical sales people.

H. They go together, laddy. Actors are sales people – they're selling themselves, and that great illusion we call theatre. Funnily enough, I'm off to the theatre today to meet an agent – one of Britain's best. He wants to **computerize** his whole operation and I believe ERGO has just the product for him. **Care to come along?**

S. Er ist unser stellvertretender Geschäftsführer.

H. Oh, dann sollte ich **besser aufpassen,** nicht wahr?

S. Keine Sorge, Hamilton. Ich habe Peter auf dem Weg von Glasgow hierher genau ins Bild gesetzt – und ihm erzählt, dass Sie einer unserer besten aber auch theatralischsten Verkäufer sind.

H. Das beides passt gut zusammen, Freundchen. Schauspieler sind auch Verkäufer – sie verkaufen sich selbst und die großartige Illusion, die wir Theater nennen. Komischerweise gehe ich heute tatsächlich zum Theater, um mich mit einem Künstleragenten zu treffen – einem der besten in England. Er will sein ganzes Geschäft **auf Computer umstellen** und glaubt, dass ERGO genau das richtige Produkt für ihn hat. **Möchten Sie nicht mitkommen?**

Background Information

In this section of the dialogue Hamilton asks Steve, Angus and Peter if they would **care** to join him in his meeting with his agent. »**Care**« here means **to like**. One can say, »I don't care for this wine very much« or »Would you care to come to a concert tonight?« etc.
»**To take care**« means **to pay attention** or **to be careful** and one can also **take care of somebody**, meaning **to look after him/her**. The opposite of **careful** is **careless**.
»**To care (about)**« can also mean **to be interested in** or **sympathetic towards something**, e.g. »She really cares about the environment«.

To return to the original example, »**Care to come along?**« is a suggestion. Other ways to suggest something using the same verb phrase »come along«, include (in order of formality, the most formal first):

a) Would you like to come along?
b) Why don't you come along?
c) Let's go together.
d) How about you coming along?
e) Do you fancy coming along?

Notice how the first three examples use the verb in the infinitive, whereas (c) and (d) have the verb in the gerund (-ing).

 Train Yourself

Setzen Sie nun das Verb in Klammern entweder in den Infinitiv oder die Gerundform!

1. Hi Larry. Do you fancy _____ (join) me for lunch tomorrow?
2. Why don't you _____ (speak) to him first on the telephone and then we'll arrange a meeting?
3. Would you care to _____ (meet) me in the bar for a drink?
4. Let's _____ (make) an arrangement to go over the plans next week, shall we?
5. OK, Peter, how about you _____ (start) off the meeting today?
6. Would you like to _____ (attend) the conference with me as my P.A.?
7. Why don't we _____ (break) off for lunch now, I'm starving!
8. Do you fancy _____ (share) a bottle of the Beaujolais? It's an excellent year.

 **Talk Talk Talk**

(In the City Theatre)

H. Here we are – the City Theatre. You know, of course, Peter, about our Edinburgh Festival?

P. Yes, indeed. I always wanted to go but somehow never got the chance.

H. You'll have to wait till next year now – the Festival has just closed. Darryl Thomas, the famous theatrical agent, stayed behind to discuss this **possible contract**. We're meeting him in the General Manager's office …

H. Hello, Darryl – good to see you again! Did you enjoy the festival?

D. I did indeed, and it has **alerted me to** a lot of latent talent. I've got a lot to do.

H. Then let's not waste our time. Oh, let me introduce you to two colleagues from London …

D. ERGO are really here in force,

(Im *City Theatre*)

H. Da wären wir – das *City Theatre*. Ich vermute, Sie kennen unser Edinburgh Festival, Peter?

P. Ja, sicher. Ich wollte immer schon einmal hingehen, aber ich hatte noch nie die Gelegenheit.

H. Dann werden Sie jetzt bis zum nächsten Jahr warten müssen – das Festival ist gerade zu Ende gegangen. Darryl Thomas, der berühmte Theateragent, ist noch geblieben, um über den **möglichen Geschäftsabschluss** zu reden. Wir treffen uns mit ihm im Büro des General Managers …

H. Hallo, Darryl – schön, Sie wieder zu sehen! Hat Ihnen das Festival gefallen?

D. Allerdings, und **ich bin** dabei auf eine Menge schlummernde Talente **aufmerksam geworden**. Es wird viel für mich zu tun geben …

H. Dann sollten wir keine Zeit mehr verschwenden. Oh, darf ich Ihnen zwei Kollegen aus London vorstellen …

D. ERGO ist ja wirklich massiv

then. Am I such an **important catch** for you?

H. Darryl, you are so important that I've drawn up a **special deal**. This software has been practically **custom-made** for you and your company's **requirements**. Let me explain ...

vertreten. Bin ich denn wirklich so ein **wichtiger Fang** für Sie?

H. Darryl, Sie sind so wichtig, dass ich für Sie ein **Spezialangebot** entworfen habe. Diese Software wurde quasi für Sie und die **Ansprüche** Ihrer Firma **maßgeschneidert**. Lassen Sie mich das erklären ...

False Friends

Peter is very **interested** in going to the Edinburgh festival and he is probably **disappointed** that he will have to wait until next year. »**Interested**« and »**disappointed**« are past participles of the verbs »**to interest**« and »**to disappoint**« as in »They disappointed me when they cancelled the meeting«, or »The new book on business techniques really interested him«.

»**Disappointed**« and »**interested**« describe how one feels about something, one's emotions.

Of course one can also use the same stems as adjectives, i.e. »**interesting**« and »**disappointing**« which describe nouns but not a person's feelings. Thus, it is possible to say »I am bored with this class« but not »I am boring with this class«. Similarly, »The book is fascinating« but not »The book is fascinated.«

Background Information

Let's look at some pairs of past participles and adjectives commonly used in English:

interesting	interested
boring	bored
disappointing	disappointed
fascinating	fascinated
tiring	tired

worrying	worried
exciting	excited
confusing	confused
annoying	annoyed
frustrating	frustrated

 Train Yourself

Wählen Sie das richtige Wort aus der Klammer:

1. The seminar on sales techniques was _____ (fascinating/fascinated).
2. It was very _____ (disappointing/disappointed) to lose the sale after all the work we put in.
3. We found the new proposals for the planned takeover quite _____ (confusing/confused).
4. After the _____ (tiring/tired) journey I was ready for my bed.
5. All of the shareholders were terribly _____ (exciting/excited) at the news of the merger.
6. The effect on business of global communications via the internet is _____ (fascinating/fascinated).
7. My God! I've never been so _____ (bored/boring) in all my life! I thought his speech would never end!
8. There's no point _____ (worrying/worried) about what may or may not happen. To succeed one must take some risks.
9. I was incredibly _____ (annoying/annoyed) when I found out that my work had been accidentally erased from the computer.
10. There are some very _____ (interesting/interested) theories on effective business management in this book I am reading at the moment.

 **Talk Talk Talk**

(Still in the theatre)

H. ... so you see, the system gives you a completely reliable **data base**. It gives a new dimension to the term »**multi-media**« because we are adding the element »theatre« to it. You can **put on file** not only the contents of your clients' **personal portfolios** but even video excerpts from roles they have played. You can download onto your **mini-digital PC** for use when you are on the road or attending festivals, or you can go directly online with it, delivering far more information to producers, directors and theatre managers than was ever possible by **conventional means**.

D. I like it, I do confess. But it's hideously expensive. I could **revamp** my whole office and take on an **extra pair of hands** for that price.

H. Darryl, I said you were an important client for us, and **I've drawn up a deal you can't refuse**. We **install the system**, you use it for six months, completely **free of charge**. If at the end of the six months you like it then you keep it

(Immer noch im Theater)

H. ... wie Sie sehen, garantiert Ihnen das System eine absolut verlässliche **Datenbank**. Es fügt dem Begriff »**Multi-Media**« eine völlig neue Dimension hinzu, da es über ein »theatralisches« Element erweitert ist. Sie können damit nicht nur **Daten** über Ihre Klienten **abspeichern**, sondern sogar Video-Ausschnitte der Rollen hinzufügen, die sie gespielt haben. Sie können das Ganze auf ihren **Mini-Digital-PC** herunterladen, wenn Sie unterwegs sind oder Festivals besuchen oder Sie können damit direkt online gehen und mehr Informationen an Produzenten, Regisseure oder Theatermanager weiterleiten, als es mit **konventionellen Mitteln** bisher möglich war.

D. Ich muss zugeben, es gefällt mir, aber es ist furchtbar teuer. Ich könnte für diesen Preis mein ganzes Büro **neu einrichten** und eine **zusätzliche Hilfskraft** einsetzen.

H. Darryl, ich habe ja gesagt, dass Sie ein wichtiger Klient für uns sind und **ich habe Ihnen ein Angebot zusammengestellt, dass Sie nicht ablehnen können**. Wir **installieren** Ihnen das **System** und Sie können es sechs Monate lang völlig **kosten-**

and, if you like, take advantage of our **extended payments plan**. If you don't like it, then **we'll just pick it up and shake hands**. But, in that case, I want a bundle of tickets for next year's Edinburgh Festival. Now is that a deal – or is that not a deal?

los benutzen. Wenn es Ihnen nach Ablauf der sechs Monate gefallen hat, können Sie es behalten und wenn Sie wollen auf unseren **Ratenzahlungsplan** zurückgreifen. Wenn es Ihnen nicht gefällt, **nehmen wir es einfach zurück und sind quitt**. Aber in diesem Fall will ich ein ganzes Bündel Tickets für das Edinburgh Festival im nächsten Jahr. Ist das ein Angebot oder nicht?

D. You old ham, Hamilton! I said I like it – now let me think about it. How long are you in Edinburgh?

D. Hamilton, Sie alter Schurke (eigentlich: Schmierenkomödiant!). Ich sagte doch, es gefällt mir – jetzt lassen Sie mich darüber nachdenken. Wie lange sind Sie in Edinburgh?

H. Just as long as it takes for you to make up your mind, Darryl laddy.

H. So lange, wie Sie brauchen, bis Sie sich entschieden haben, Darryl, alter Freund.

D. Look, there's a very fine Festival production which has extended its run at the Prince's Theatre. I'll get you tickets – it'll **give** Peter **an insight** into contemporary British theatre, unless London has already given him that.

D. Hören Sie, in der Verlängerung läuft noch eine exzellente Festival-Aufführung im *Prince's Theatre*. Ich werde Ihnen Tickets besorgen – es wird Peter **einen Einblick** in das zeitgenössische, britische Theater **geben**, wenn er den in London noch nicht bekommen hat.

P. I just haven't had the time, I do confess.

P. Ich muss zugeben, dass ich noch nicht die Zeit dazu hatte.

D. Then off you go tonight to the theatre. I'll give you a call at your hotel tomorrow morning. Agreed?

D. Dann heißt es für Sie heute Abend: auf ins Theater. Ich werde Sie morgen früh in Ihrem Hotel anrufen. Einverstanden?

Background Information

Darryl says to Peter that going to a play in Edinburgh will **give him an insight** into contemporary British theatre. **»An insight«** is **a clear understanding of a complex problem or situation**. Let's look at some other »sight« words and expressions:

foresight	the ability to judge what is going to happen in the future and plan one's actions based on this knowledge
hindsight	the ability to understand why or how something was done in the past and how it might have been done better
at first sight	when first seen
to lose sight of	to not pay attention to something or forget about
to be within sight	to be almost finished
to go sightseeing	to visit interesting places usually when on holiday
to set one's sights on	to try very hard to achieve something

Train Yourself

Füllen Sie die Lücken der folgenden Sätze!

1. After spending two days working on the report the end was _____ .
2. I had no time to _____ when I was in Copenhagen, all I saw was the office and my hotel room.
3. I think we've _____ of our initial goal to sell software of high quality at a price people can afford.
4. Paul had _____ being Company Director within ten years and was therefore devastated when he heard he'd been passed over for promotion.

5. In ▨▨▨▨▨▨▨▨, we should have moved in to secure the contract earlier and then we wouldn't have lost out to Farrell and Sons.
6. Spending a month being shown around the various departments of the company will give you an ▨▨▨▨▨▨▨▨ into how things work round here.
7. Charles had the ▨▨▨▨▨▨▨▨ to sell his shares in the company long before the crash occurred.
8. ▨▨▨▨▨▨▨▨ the plan seemed to be full of holes but after consideration, we decided to go ahead with it.

 Talk Talk Talk

(The hotel. At breakfast)

A. Good morning, gentlemen. Slept well?

S. and P.: Very well, Angus. What's on the programme today?

A. The waiting game – waiting for Darryl's call. Actually, let's **take the morning off** and look around Edinburgh. You've never seen the city, Peter – it's a northern city but I'm sure quite unlike your Hamburg.

P. I'd love to see around the city. I've read so much about it, of course.

S. Then off we go after breakfast.

(Im Hotel, beim Frühstück)

A. Guten Morgen, meine Herren. Gut geschlafen?

S. und P.: Sehr gut, Angus. Was steht heute auf dem Programm?

A. Das übliche Warten – auf Darryls Anruf. Lassen Sie uns einfach **den Morgen frei nehmen** und uns Edinburgh ansehen. Sie haben die Stadt ja noch nie gesehen, Peter – es ist eine Stadt des Nordens, aber ganz sicher anders als Ihr Hamburg.

P. Ich würde mir die Stadt liebend gern ansehen. Ich habe natürlich schon viel darüber gelesen.

S. Dann ziehen wir gleich nach

I'll call Hamilton – he can **double as a guide** for us. Angus, you'll be wanting to get back to Glasgow.

A. I've a lot waiting for me there, that's for sure. If you don't need me any more I'll **get on the road**.

(Later, on Edinburgh's Prince's Street)

P. Look, isn't that Melissa over there?

S. Good lord, yes. What's she doing here? I didn't know she intended coming to Scotland. Hey, Melissa.

M. Heavens above, what are you two boys doing in Edinburgh? You're supposed to be in Glasgow.

S. That was yesterday, Melissa. We're working. What are you up to?

M. **Secret assignment** – but I'll tell you later.

S. Over lunch?

M. Yes, why not.

dem Frühstück los. Ich rufe Hamilton an – er kann für uns auch den **Fremdenführer spielen**. Angus, Sie werden sicher zurück nach Glasgow fahren wollen.

A. Dort wartet wirklich genug Arbeit auf mich, so viel ist sicher. Wenn Sie mich nicht mehr brauchen, **mache** ich **mich** wieder **auf den Weg**.

(Später, auf der *Prince's Street* in Edinburgh)

P. Sehen Sie mal, ist das da drüben nicht Melissa?

S. Guter Gott, ja. Was macht sie denn hier? Ich wusste gar nicht, dass sie vorgehabt hatte, nach Schottland zu fahren. Hey, Melissa.

M. Du lieber Himmel, was macht ihr zwei Jungs denn in Edinburgh? Solltet Ihr nicht in Glasgow sein?

S. Das war gestern, Melissa. Wir arbeiten. Was machen Sie denn hier?

M. Ein **geheimer Auftrag** – aber ich werde es Ihnen später erzählen.

S. Beim Mittagessen?

M. Ja, warum nicht.

S. At our hotel then. It's the Connaught ...	S. Dann treffen wir uns in unserem Hotel. Es ist das Connaught ...
(At the hotel)	(Im Hotel)
Receptionist: You had a call from a Mr McGregor, sir.	Empfangsdame: Ein Mr. McGregor hat für Sie angerufen, Sir.
S. That'll be to say Darryl has given his answer. I'll call right away ... Hamilton? Any news. He did? He has? That's great ... Peter, Ham **made the sale**. That's a **real feather in ERGO's cap**. Now to lunch - here's Melissa.	S. Wahrscheinlich wollte er uns mitteilen, dass Darryl ihm eine Antwort gegeben hat. Ich rufe gleich zurück ... Hamilton? Gibt es etwas Neues? Hat er? Er hat? Das ist ja großartig ... Peter, Ham **hat das Geschäft abgeschlossen**. Das ist ein **schöner Erfolg für ERGO**. Jetzt auf zum Mittagessen – da ist Melissa schon.
(At lunch)	(Beim Mittagessen)
S. Well, Melissa, what's this secret you're withholding from us?	S. Also, Melissa, was für ein Geheimnis verbergen Sie vor uns?
M. I don't know how to tell you two boys this, but I'm leaving ERGO to come up here and work. It wasn't an easy decision, but the offer was too good to **turn down**.	M. Ich weiß gar nicht, wie ich euch beiden Jungs das beibringen soll, aber ich verlasse ERGO, um hier zu arbeiten. Es war keine leichte Entscheidung, aber das Angebot war zu gut, um **»Nein« sagen** zu können.
P. I'm very sorry indeed to hear that Melissa.	P. Es tut mir wirklich Leid, das zu hören, Melissa.
S. So will James. When do you leave, Melissa?	S. So wird es James auch ergehen. Wann verlassen Sie uns, Melissa?

M. In about six weeks.	M. In etwa sechs Wochen.
S. Just time enough to complete your marketing programme for the **trade fair**. At least, you'll be seeing a lot of her on that project, Peter. Don't look so crestfallen. In this game you win one and lose one ...	S. Gerade genug Zeit, um Ihr Marketing-Programm für die **Messe** fertig zu stellen. Wenigstens werden Sie sie bei diesem Projekt häufig sehen, Peter. Also schauen Sie nicht wie ein begossener Pudel. Mal gewinnt man in diesem Spiel, mal verliert man ...

Background Information

Melissa tells her colleagues in this section of the dialogue that she had an offer of work that was too good to **turn down**. »**To turn down**« is **to refuse or reject something or someone**. Let's look at some more expressions with »**turn**«.

to turn out	to happen in the end
to turn up (a)	to arrive
to turn up (b)	to discover by chance
to turn around	to cause a situation or organisation to improve
to turn in	to go to bed
turnover	the amount of business a company does in a period of time
to take turns	a number of people do the same thing one after the other

Train Yourself

Benutzen Sie diese Wendungen in den unten stehenden Sätzen!

1. The company's annual ▒▒▒▒▒▒▒▒▒▒ has been increasing every year.
2. On the way to the conference we ▒▒▒▒▒▒▒▒▒▒ with the driving so that nobody got too tired.

3. The new Chief Executive brought in new measures to try and ▬▬▬▬▬▬▬▬ the company's fortunes after a very disappointing year.
4. In the end everything ▬▬▬▬▬▬▬▬ fine and the deadline was met.
5. On business trips abroad I usually ▬▬▬▬▬▬▬▬ quite early so as to be fresh next day.
6. The candidate did himself no favours by ▬▬▬▬▬▬▬▬ late for the interview and wasting the interviewer's time.
7. The company ▬▬▬▬▬▬▬▬ the offer as it was felt it wouldn't be beneficial for the shareholders in the long-term future.
8. After searching all morning for my car keys they finally ▬▬▬▬▬▬▬▬ behind the sofa.

Vocabulary

business centre	Handelszentrum
Care to come along?	Möchten Sie nicht mitkommen?
to computerize	auf Computer umstellen
conventional means	konventionelle Mittel
custom-made	maßgeschneidert
data base	Datenbank
to double as a guide	den Fremdenführer spielen
to draw up	entwerfen, zusammenstellen
easily accessible	leicht zugänglich
electronic commerce	elektronischer Handel
extended payments plan	Ratenzahlungsplan
free of charge	kostenlos
to get on the road	sich auf den Weg machen
to give an insight	einen Einblick geben
grapevine	Gerüchteküche *(fig.)*
hand	Hilfskraft
highly-qualified	hochqualifiziert
high-tech age	Zeitalter der Hochtechnologie
to intrigue	sehr interessieren
to make a sale	ein Geschäft abschließen
marketing material	Werbematerial

personal approach	persönlicher Ansatz
pool of labour	Arbeitskräfte
to pull in	anhalten
to revamp	neu einrichten
secret assignment	Geheimauftrag
sidekick (Am.)	Partner, Kumpel (ugs.)
special deal	Spezialangebot
springing up all over the place	überall aus dem Boden schießen
to take off	frei nehmen
to turn down	ablehnen
trade fair	Handelsmesse
virtual marketplace	virtuelle Verkaufsstellen
visual presentation	visuelle Präsentation
website	Website

The Test - How good are you now in sales talk?

Below are thirty multiple choice sentences using vocabulary and structures we have looked at in this book.

Finden Sie die richtigen Lösungen zu den Sätzen und ergänzen Sie sie!

1. Our foreign visitors were ▮▮▮▮▮ *(put down/put by/put up)* in the Brighton Hotel.

2. Tony was looking forward ▮▮▮▮▮ *(by/to/in)* meeting the new Sales Director.

3. Before putting the product on the market it was tried ▮▮▮▮▮ *(out/by/over)* on over a thousand people.

4. The new publicity campaign really made ▮▮▮▮▮ *(amends/a difference/a bid)* for the previous disastrous campaign.

5. You get in touch with Mr Greaves and in the ▮▮▮▮▮ *(meantime/meanwhile/meaning)* I'll try and find his contract.

6. Have a guess who I ran ▮▮▮▮▮ *(down/by/into)* last week? George Partridge.

7. The Managing Director finished his speech by asking if ▮▮▮▮▮ *(anyone/someone/no-one)* had any questions.

8. Beryl was the ▮▮▮▮▮ *(mainframe/mainstay/mainstream)* of the company and made sure everything ran smoothly.

9. Peter was new ▮▮▮▮▮ *(on/over/to)* the job and therefore was worried ▮▮▮▮▮ *(about/in/to)* his performance.

10. It is important to be _____ (privately/unfailingly/warmly) polite when dealing with a new client.

11. We were held _____ (up/down/by) traffic and arrived at the conference two hours late.

12. Sales figures were _____ (completely/slightly/remarkably) higher than last quarter but head office were still not happy.

13. _____ (In the meantime/From time to time/In the nick of time) I do research on my chosen subject but not as much as I should do.

14. On arriving at the hotel the _____ (receptionist/receiver/receptive) showed us where our rooms were.

15. I went _____ (by/over/to) the report three times before I found the error.

16. Management are currently _____ (looking into/seeking out/searching for) the possibility of opening a new branch in Glasgow.

17. We must persuade possible investors that it is worth _____ (doing/their weight in gold/their while) to put money into our company.

18. Operator: Can you _____ (hold/get/put) the line, please? He's in a meeting at the moment.

19. We had to pay through the _____ (mouth/nose/ear) to rent out the conference hall.

20. There was a _____ (breakdown/breakup/break-off) in communications between the two sides and the matter had to got to an industrial tribunal.

21. Right from the start there was something very _____ (upper hand/red-handed/ underhand) about the entire process.

22. The company finally got the project _____ (on/out/off) the ground after months of debating.

23. Bankruptcy was _____ (staring us in the face/face to face with us/facing up to us) and therefore we had to call in the receiver.

24. If we want to compete effectively in the marketplace we _____ (will have to/will have had to/are having to) transform our entire corporate structure.

25. Tony was the star of the company after pulling _____ (off/out/around) a great victory in securing increased revenue for ERGO Ltd.

26. I found the trade fair _____ (fascinating/fascinated) but became extremely _____ (boring/bored) on the way home.

27. After the end of the recent economic crisis there was a noticeable _____ (turnover/turnaround/turndown) in the company's fortunes.

28. _____ (How's things/How's life/How do you do), Mr Jones? It's a great pleasure to meet the Senior Director of Jennings Ltd.

29. This computer has _____ (seen better days/gone one better/bettered). We must order a new one.

30. _____ (Would/Do/Can) you mind I'm trying to work here!

Ready for sales talk

1. Produkte präsentieren

Ladies and gentlemen, we are gathered here today to listen to Mrs Walker's presentation on ...	Meine Damen und Herren, wir haben uns heute hier versammelt, um Frau Walkers Präsentation über ... zu hören.
It is my pleasure to introduce our guest, Mrs Walker, to you.	Es ist mir eine Freude, Ihnen unseren Gast, Frau Walker, vorzustellen.
We are pleased to have Mr Brückner as our guest.	Wir freuen uns, Herrn Brückner als unseren Gast zu haben.
Could you please hold back all questions and comments until after I am done?	Könnten Sie bitte alle Fragen und Anmerkungen zurückhalten bis ich meinen Vortrag beendet habe.
Please feel free to interrupt me any time.	Falls irgendwelche Fragen aufkommen, scheuen Sie sich bitte nicht, mich zu unterbrechen.
There will be enough time for questions and comments after the presentation.	Im Anschluss an die Präsentation wird genug Zeit für Fragen sein.
After the first half of the presentation there will be a break of ten minutes.	Nach der ersten Hälfte der Präsentation wird es eine Pause von zehn Minuten geben.
I will begin my presentation by giving you an overview of ...	Ich werde meine Präsentation damit beginnen, Ihnen einen Überblick über ... zu geben.

We will use transparencies to present the facts.	Wir werden Folien verwenden, um die Sachverhalte darzustellen.
To show you ... I have brought some slides.	Um Ihnen ... zu zeigen, habe ich einige Dias mitgebracht.
This short film will introduce you to ...	Dieser kurze Film wird Sie mit ... vertraut machen.
I have brought a video to demonstrate ...	Ich habe ein Video mitgebracht, um zu zeigen ...

2. Kunden überzeugen

I think that/ I believe that ...	Ich denke/ glaube, dass ...
I am sure/ certain that ...	Ich bin sicher, dass ...
I am absolutely sure that ...	Ich bin absolut sicher, dass ...
In my opinion ...	Meiner Ansicht nach ...
From my point of view ...	Nach meiner Auffassung ...
In my eyes ...	In meinen Augen ...
I presume/assume that ...	Ich nehme an / vermute, dass ...
As I see it ...	So wie ich das sehe ...
I am persuaded that ...	Ich bin überzeugt, dass ...
I am positive that ...	Ich bin mir ganz sicher, dass ...
The first reason for this I would like to mention is ...	Der erste Grund hierfür, den ich erwähnen möchte, ist ...
Second/Secondly there is ... to talk about.	Zweitens sollten wir über ... sprechen.
In addition, we shouldn't forget that ...	Zusätzlich sollten wir nicht vergessen, dass ...
Furthermore ...	Ferner/Des Weiteren ...
Moreover ...	Darüber hinaus ...
I would like to add ...	Ich würde gerne ... hinzufügen.
Not only ... but also ...	Nicht nur ... sondern auch ...
On the one hand ... on the other hand ...	Einerseits ... andererseits ...
In general ...	Im allgemeinen ...

Generally speaking ...	Allgemein gesprochen ...
On the whole ...	Im Großen und Ganzen ...
All in all ...	Alles in allem ...
Nevertheless I should not forget to mention ...	Nichtsdestotrotz sollte ich nicht vergessen zu erwähnen ...
In spite of ...	Trotz ...
Despite the fact that ...	Trotz der Tatsache, dass ...
However ...	Aber/Trotzdem/Jedoch ...
Although ...	Obwohl ...
Instead of ...	Statt/Anstatt ...
Instead, ...	Stattdessen ...
Therefore ...	Deshalb/Deswegen
For that reason ...	Darum/Aus diesem Grund

3. Sie sind noch nicht ganz überzeugt!

I am not quite convinced.	Ich bin nicht ganz davon überzeugt.
I am not quite sure if I can agree.	Ich bin nicht ganz sicher, ob ich dem zustimmen kann.
What if you are wrong?	Was ist, wenn Sie sich irren?
I am afraid I cannot follow your argument.	Leider verstehe ich nicht, was Sie sagen wollen.
Could you please go more into detail?	Könnten Sie bitte mehr ins Detail gehen?
It might be better if ...	Es wäre vielleicht besser, wenn ...
Why don't you tell us more about ...?	Warum erzählen Sie uns nicht mehr zu ...?
I wonder if you have taken into account that ...	Ich frage mich, ob Sie berücksichtigt haben, dass ...

Excuse me, Madam (Sir), may I interrupt you?	Entschuldigen Sie, darf ich Sie unterbrechen?
Sorry to break in, but ...	Tut mir Leid, dass ich Sie unterbreche, aber ...
Excuse me, may I ask you a question?	Entschuldigen Sie, darf ich Ihnen eine Frage stellen?
If I might just add something?	Wenn ich dazu etwas hinzufügen dürfte?
Before coming to a hasty decision we should leave it here.	Bevor wir zu einer übereilten Entscheidung kommen, sollten wir es hierbei belassen.
I am sorry, it is impossible to accept this offer.	Es tut mir Leid, das Angebot können wir nicht annehmen.
There seems to have been some slight misunderstanding. Could you please go back to your first point and clarify it?	Hier scheint ein kleines Missverständnis vorzuliegen. Würden Sie bitte Ihren ersten Punkt noch einmal erläutern?
We still have our doubts about ...	Wir haben immer noch Zweifel an ...
I am afraid that I cannot share your point of view.	Ihre Ansicht kann ich leider nicht teilen.

4. Vertragsbedingungen aushandeln

Would you be prepared to accept this offer?	Wären Sie bereit, dieses Angebot anzunehmen?
Provided that ..., I will accept your conditions.	Vorausgesetzt, dass ..., werde ich Ihre Bedingungen akzeptieren.

To be honest, don't you think that his suggestion is more realistic?	Um ehrlich zu sein, denken Sie nicht, dass sein Vorschlag realistischer ist?
I still have to reject your offer.	Ich muß Ihr Angebot immer noch zurückweisen.
This is my last offer.	Das ist mein letztes Angebot.
I can see what you mean, but I still think ...	Ich verstehe was Sie meinen, aber trotzdem denke ich ...
I am afraid we cannot support your proposal.	Leider können wir Ihren Vorschlag nicht unterstützen.
Unfortunately we have to reject your offer.	Leider müssen wir Ihr Angebot ablehnen.
Would this be satisfactory for you?	Wäre das für Sie zufrieden stellend?
Would you be prepared to accept this offer?	Wären Sie bereit, dieses Angebot anzunehmen?

5. Abschlüsse erzielen

Wouldn't it be better if we tried to settle on a compromise?	Wäre es nicht besser, zu versuchen, uns auf einen Kompromiss zu einigen?
If you don't try to understand our point of view, we will not be willing to strike a compromise.	Wenn Sie nicht versuchen, unseren Standpunkt zu verstehen, werden wir nicht bereit sein, einen Kompromiss zu finden.
No, we will not support this compromise.	Nein, wir werden diesen Kompromiss nicht unterstützen.

What about leaving the differences aside and finding a solution.	Wie wäre es, wenn wir die Meinungsverschiedenheiten beiseite ließen und eine Lösung fänden?
This should be negotiable, don't you think?	Darüber sollten wir verhandeln können, denken Sie nicht ?
I am afraid that we cannot come to an agreement.	Ich fürchte, wir können zu keiner Übereinstimmung kommen.
This sounds good to me and I think I can accept it.	Das klingt gut und ich denke, ich kann es akzeptieren.
Good then, I will accept your suggestion.	Also gut, ich werde Ihren Vorschlag annehmen.
I am glad that we found a common solution.	Ich bin froh, dass wir eine gemeinsame Lösung gefunden haben.
I see that we have come to an agreement.	Ich sehe, wir sind uns einig.

Glossary

a broad palette	eine breite Palette
to buzz	etwas brummt (vor Besuchern)/ hat Pep
account credit	Kreditkonten
accounting program	Abrechnungsprogramm
accounting system	Buchhaltungssystem
to adopt an approach	einen Ansatz benutzen
advance	Fortschritt
advanced technology	fortschrittliche Technologie
agenda	Tagesordnung
agent	Vertreter
a lot of scope	ein breites Betätigungsfeld
an important catch	ein wichtiger Fang
appointment	Termin, Verabredung
assistant managing director	stellvertretender Geschäftsführer
beforehand	im Voraus
to be in the market for	wirklich Bedarf haben nach
to be out of s.o.'s league	Spezialgebiet von jdm. sein
to better	verbessern
to book	buchen
booking	Reservierung
brand	Marke
to break	unterbrechen
broadband communications	Breitband-Kommunikation
business area	Geschäftsgebiet, Geschäftsfeld
business centre	Handelszentrum
Care to come along?	Möchten Sie nicht mitkommen?
to carry s.o.'s range	jds. Sortiment übernehmen
to catch s.o.'s attention	jds. Aufmerksamkeit erregen
chief executive	Hauptgeschäftsführer
client	Kunde
client details	Kundendaten
to come in on the ground floor	von Anfang an zusammenarbeiten
commission (basis)	Provisions(rate)
competition	Konkurrenz

143

competitors' products	Konkurrenzprodukte
to computerize	auf Computer umstellen
confab	Geplauder/eine »Expertenrunde« (umgangssprachlich)
consensus	Übereinstimmung, Konsens
consultancy basis	beratende Funktion
consumer-orientated	konsumentenorientiert
conventional means	konventionelle Mittel
counter-productive	kontraproduktiv
cost-effective	kosteneffektiv
cost estimate	Kostenvoranschlag
custom-made	maßgeschneidert
data base	Datenbank
deal	Geschäft; Angebot
to demonstrate the effectiveness	die Wirksamkeit vorführen
devolution	Dezentralisierung
to double as a guide	den Fremdenführer spielen
Down to business.	Kommen wir zum Geschäftlichen.
to draw up	entwerfen, zusammenstellen
to drop	hier: fallen lassen (eine Tätigkeit stehen und liegen lassen/ auch: eine Bemerkung fallen lassen etc.)
easily accessible	leicht zugänglich
easy-going	unkompliziert
electronic commerce	elektronischer Handel
enciphered data	verschlüsselte Daten
to expand	expandieren
extended payments plan	Ratenzahlungsplan
to fall down on s.o.'s promises	jds. Versprechungen nicht nachkommen
to fall for	sich verlieben
far afield	weit weg
to fill sb. in	jdn. ins Bild setzen/ aufklären über etw.
financial exchange software	Bilanzierungsprogramm
financial services company	Finanzdienstleister
to fire away	losschießen (umgangssprachlich)

first-hand experience	eigene Erfahrungen
to follow up	folgen lassen, auch: Verfolgung
free of charge	kostenlos
to gather	hier: gehört haben
geared up	in Erwartung/voll ausgestattet
to get double value from sth.	von etw. doppelt profitieren
to get down to sth.	etw. angehen
to get hold of sth.	etw. in die Finger bekommen
to get on the road	sich auf den Weg machen
to get sth. off the ground	etw. in Gang bringen
to give an insight	einen Einblick geben
to go about sth.	etw. angehen
to go for sth.	etw. vorziehen
grapevine	»Gerüchteküche«
guinea-pig	Meerschweinchen, oft im Sinne von »Versuchskaninchen«
to hand out	ausgeben, verteilen
hand	Hilfskraft
to get sth. off the ground	etwas in Gang bringen
to handle	umgehen mit
to have time	Zeit haben
highly-qualified	hochqualifiziert
high-tech age	Zeitalter der Hochtechnologie
Honesty pays in selling!	Ehrlichkeit zahlt sich im Verkauf aus!
How's business?	Wie gehen die Geschäfte?
to immerse oneself	sich in etwas versenken; intensiv vertraut machen
in a heck of a state	in einem furchtbaren Zustand
to increase at an encouraging rate	hohe Zuwachsraten verzeichnen
to intrigue	sehr interessieren
introductory pamphlet	kurze Einführung
It will take some selling.	Es wird einige harte Verkaufsgespräche geben.
to kindle interest	Interesse entfachen
kippers	Bücklinge
to know the scene	sich auskennen
leader	hier: Marktführer
lucrative	lukrativ

mainframe	Computersystem
to make a big bid	sich sehr bemühen
to make a sale	ein Geschäft abschließen
to make out a very good case for buying sth.	ein sehr gutes Argument dafür anbringen, etw. zu kaufen
to make straight for	sich sofort aufmachen zu
to market	vermarkten
marketing material	Werbematerial
to match perfectly	perfekt passen
to match s.o.'s claim	jds. Ansprüche erfüllen
to meet the demands	die Anforderungen erfüllen
My treat!	Das geht auf meine Rechnung!
new revolution	neue Revolution
of paramount importance	von entscheidender Bedeutung
one-man operation	Ein-Mann-Betrieb
out and about	unterwegs
packaging	Verpackung
to pay dividends	sich bezahlt machen
payment plan	Finanzplan
personal approach	persönlicher Ansatz
pool of labour	Arbeitskräfte
preliminary observations	grundlegende Feststellungen
promotional material	Promotionmaterial
to provide	bereitstellen
to pull in	anhalten
to put on file	abspeichern
reception	Empfang
retail outlet	Einzelhandels-Niederlassung
to revamp	neu einrichten
right on time	rechtzeitig
roll out the heavy guns	»schwere Geschütze auffahren«
to rubbish	abwerten
run down	erschöpft (hier: schlecht gemacht)
sale	Geschäftsabschluss
sales approach	Verkaufsstrategie
sales area	Verkaufsbereich
sales chief	Verkaufsleiter
sales director	Verkaufsleiter

sales experience	Verkaufserfahrung
salesman	Vertreter
salesmanship	Verkaufsgeschäft; Verkaufen
sales operation	Tagesaktivitäten
salespeople	hier: Außendienstmitarbeiter
salesperson	Verkäufer
sales pitch	Verkaufsargument
sales points	Verkaufsstellen
sales representative	Vertreter
sales stand	Verkaufsstand
sales strategy	Verkaufsstrategie
sales trip	Verkaufsreise
schedule	Terminkalender
secondary	zweitrangig
secondment	Abordnung, im Sinne von »jdm. unterstellt werden«
secret assignment	Geheimauftrag
to seek out	finden, heraussuchen
selling point	Verkaufsargument
seminar on salesmanship	Verkaufsseminar
to set up	sich niederlassen
to show sb. the ropes	jdm. etw. erklären (ugs.)
sidekick	Partner, Kumpel
sloppy	schlampig, nachlässig
to sort out	klassifizieren, einteilen
to sort out sth. for sb.	für jdn. etw. erklären
special deal	Spezialangebot
specifications	nähere Angaben
springing up all over the place	»überall aus dem Boden schießen«
to stick to	hier: bleiben bei
strong point	starke Seite
subsidies	Subventionen
to suit the purpose	den Anforderungen entsprechen
to tackle sth.	fertig werden mit etw.
tailored	maßgeschneidert
to take off	frei nehmen
task	Ziel
tax breaks	Steuererleichterungen

That's just the ticket.	Das ist genau das Richtige.
the gift of the gab	die Gabe einer »großen Klappe«
trade fair	Handelsmesse
trade press	Fachpresse
to turn down	ablehnen
under our belts	unter Dach und Fach
up-to-date	hochaktuell
venture	Unternehmung
virtual marketplace	virtuelle Verkaufsstellen
visual presentation	visuelle Präsentation
warehouse floor	Lager
website	Website
well aware	im Klaren darüber
What's on the agenda?	Was steht auf der Tagesordnung?
When it comes to selling ...	Wenn es darum geht ... anzupreisen
wild about	wild/verrückt nach
to win the franchise	die Konzession bekommen

Solutions

Seite
8. 1. scaling down
2. write ... down
3. bring up
4. putting ... up
5. setting up
6. let ... down
7. followed up
8. turned down
9. writing up
10. running down
11. go up
12. going down

11. 1. To visit us
2. To write to us
3. One last drink
4. A loser or a failure (He dropped out of college.)
5. To fall asleep
6. Deliver something (»Oh Tony, can you drop these letters off at the post office for me?«)

13. 1. called off
2. set off
3. pulled off
4. taken off
5. put off
6. switch off

14. 1. bargained for
2. stands for
3. put in for
4. fell for
5. makes for
6. makes up for

18. 1. prototype
2. sound ... out
3. try out
4. trial runs
5. test the water
6. guinea-pigs
7. piloting
8. samples
9. pitch

21. 1. made a point of
2. making headway
3. made a ... bid
4. made amends
5. make allowances
6. make a ... pitch
7. made a stand
8. made a case for
9. made an impact

23. 1. Let's consider offering this new product for sale.
2. Let me just think the idea over.
3. Come in, sit down and let's look over this proposal.
4. It's a fine day – let's get out the car and go for a drive into the mountains.
5. Let her fax this cost analysis to the customer right away.
6. Let the company wait another week for delivery – they are always so impatient.
7. Let me explain what we have in mind.
8. Let us join in this new venture.

26. 1. The proposal was significantly more attractive on paper than it was in practice.
2. Our marketing office is nowhere near as big as our sales office/Our sales office is nowhere near as big as our marketing office.
3. This is by far the most comprehensive business journal I have ever seen.

4. The Jones account was unquestionably the most lucrative the company had ever won.
5. Share prices remain a little lower than expected.
6. She was easily the most diligent salesperson in the company.
7. The Marlboro trademark is unquestionably the most recognised in the world.
8. The present Sales Director is much better informed than the previous incumbent.
9. It was not really as serious as we expected.

31. 1. We got there just in time.
2. correct
3. from time to time
4. in the nick of time
5. about time
6. correct
7. killing time
8. correct
9. on time
10. correct

34. 1. in receipt of
2. in receivership
3. received
4. to reciprocate
5. recipients
6. reception
7. receptive
8. receptionist
9. on the receiving end of
10. receiver

37. 1. go over ... with a fine toothcomb
2. went all out
3. goes without saying
4. make a go of
5. go it alone
6. touch and go

7. went about
8. from the word go
9. let themselves go
10. go hand in hand

40. 1. came across
2. sorting out
3. check up on
4. look ... up
5. running over
6. hunt down
7. sort ... out
8. searching for
9. look into

43. 1. The Managing Director is standing down at the end of the year.
2. — Personally I put it down to the recession.
3. At the end of the day the success of a company all comes down to the degree of efficiency in which it is run.
4. When a new manager takes over a company he must lay down the law.
5. If everybody refused to back down during negotiations no deal would ever be reached.
6. Now I think we all know each other so let`s get down to business.
7. I think we should bring down the price in order to make it more cost-effective.
8. The Advertising Standards Council promised to come down hard on any companies using underhand methods to sell their products.

46. 1. worth his salt/his weight in gold
2. worth ... while
3. for what it's worth
4. for all ... worth
5. worthy
6. make it worth your while
7. not worth the paper it's printed on
8. worthless

48. 1. John was last seen getting into a taxi.
2. The report was published last year
3. The departure time will be announced later on today.
4. Fiat cars are made in Milan.
5. The work is being typed out as we speak.
6. 10,000 units have been sold so far this month.

50. 1. im-
2. un-
3. ir-
4. in-
5. im-
6. un-
7. ir-
8. un-
9. in-

55. 1. brought about
2. pointed out
3. come about
4. borne out
5. came out
6. set about
7. fall out
8. sort out
9. missed out on
10. carried out

57. 1. a. put me through b. hold the line c. sorry, being held up d. take a message e. give him a call, give him a ring, get on the phone to him
2. f. speaking g. fire away 3. h. extension i. unavailable, otherwise engaged j. get through

60. 1. run-of-the-mill
2. run off my feet
3. ran into
4. ran an eye over

5. run its course
6. in the long run
7. run to
8. in the running
9. run up against
10. run over/run through

62. 1. stood in
2. talked me into
3. put in for
4. take it out on
5. go in for
6. let you into
7. fill ... in
8. slept in
9. ties in
10. came in for

64. 1. domain
2. In the main
3. mainstay
4. mainspring
5. mainframe
6. maintain
7. mainstream

67. 1. pleased with
2. disappointed in
3. interested in
4. wary of
5. impressed by
6. good at, bad at
7. successful in
8. skilled in
9. worried about
10. new to
11. surprised by
12. concerned about

69. 1. directly
2. private
3. warm
4. unfailing
5. anxiously
6. Obviously
7. happily
8. rapidly
9. accurate
10. polite

72. 1. hold your breath
2. hold the fort
3. held up
4. hold with
5. held forth
6. hold out
7. got hold of the wrong end of the stick
8. get hold of
9. holding its own
10. got hold of

75. 1. paid the price
2. There will be hell to pay
3. pays dividends
4. paid through the nose
5. paid lip-service
6. paid off
7. put paid to
8. pay attention

77. 1. stick to their guns
2. stuck out like a sore thumb
3. stick their oar in
4. stick-in-the-muds
5. get the wrong end of the stick
6. stick to
7. carries the big stick
8. stick our necks out

79. 1. broke
2. broke the back
3. make or break
4. break the market
5. broke even
6. break the strike

84. 1. breaking new ground
2. break the back of
3. broke the ice
4. broke down
5. break even
6. broke up
7. breaking in
8. breakthrough
9. broke off
10. break

86. 1. at first hand
2. an old hand
3. show one's hand
4. out of hand
5. knows it like the back of his hand
6. beforehand
7. put his hand to
8. goes hand in hand
9. underhand
10. have the upper hand

90. 1. correct
2. made up their minds
3. have in mind
4. speaking her mind
5. correct
6. correct
7. slipped my mind
8. in two minds

93. 1. happy hunting ground
2. get ... off the ground
3. cut the ground from under our feet
4. break new ground
5. fell on stony ground
6. has her feet firmly on the ground
7. gain ground
8. common ground
9. has ... grounds
10. covered a lot of ground

96. 1. well-connected
2. well-thought-of
3. well-timed
4. well-established
5. well-advised
6. well-appointed
7. well-versed
8. well-disposed

99. 1. thought the better of
2. has seen better days
3. go one better
4. knows the score
5. For better or worse
6. scores
7. better
8. got the better of

102. 1. talked till I was blue in the face
2. at face value
3. staring ... in the face
4. a long face
5. face the music
6. egg on my face
7. show my face
8. face the facts
9. lose face

105. 1. on the point of
2. pointing a finger
3. make a point of
4. take your point
5. pointed out
6. Not to put too fine a point on it
7. in point of fact
8. beside the point

107. 1. Inform yourself fully about our accounting program, and let's meet over lunch tomorrow to discuss the system further. Let's then visit your office to show you the program at work.
2. a. pamphlet
   b. staff
   c. an account
   d. operation
   e. retail

112. 1. might have to
2. will have to
3. have to/must
4. has had to
5. have to/must
6. had had to
7. should have to
8. had to
9. going to have to
10. will have to

115. 1. get together
2. getting on
3. get round
4. get through to
5. get away with
6. got by
7. get over
8. get … over

118. 1. pulls his socks up
2. pulling ... weight
3. pulling ... legs
4. a) pulled out b) pull in/up
5. pulled ... off
6. pull in ... belts
7. pulled the carpet from under our feet
8. pulled out all the stops

121. 1. joining
2. speak
3. meet
4. make
5. starting
6. attend
7. break
8. sharing

124. 1. fascinating
2. disappointing
3. confusing
4. tiring
5. excited
6. fascinating
7. bored
8. worrying
9. annoyed
10. interesting

127. 1. in sight
2. go sightseeing
3. lost sight
4. set his sights on
5. hindsight
6. insight
7. foresight
8. At first sight

131. 1. turnover
2. took turns
3. turn around
4. turned out
5. turn in
6. turning up
7. turned down 8. turned up

Lösungen zum Abschlusstest
1. put up
2. to
3. out
4. amends
5. meantime
6. into
7. anyone
8. mainstay
9. to, about
10. unfailingly
11. up
12. slightly
13. from time to time
14. receptionist
15. over
16. looking into
17. their while
18. hold
19. nose
20. breakdown
21. underhand
22. off
23. staring us in the face
24. will have to
25. off
26. fascinating, bored
27. turnaround
28. How do you do
29. seen better days
30. do